LAW OF THE LAND

A Practical Legal Guide for Tourists and Business Travelers

Italy

By Michael L. Moore Esq.

DEDICATION

This book is dedicated to the memory of my late older brother, Kenneth Lee Moore, whose tragic murder at 15 years of age, inspired me to write this series of books.

This book is also dedicated to my parents, John Henry Moore, and Edna Mae Moore, whose tremendous parenting skills kept me focused on the important things in life: being reverent, getting educated, and prioritizing family.

Finally, this book is dedicated to my beautiful family, my wife Royellen, my son AJ, and my daughter Karla. They inspire me every single day to be kind, patient, and compassionate.

IN LOVING MEMORY OF:

Belinda Joyce Moore Moss-my beautiful and wonderful sister, who supported me in every positive thing that I ever attempted to do.

Michael Eugene Baker-my dedicated and loyal friend and brother who always wanted the very best for me.

Sylvia Joyce Hill—my eldest sister, who had a beautiful spirit and was like a second mother to me.

LAW OF THE LAND®

PUBLISHING for Tourists & Business Travelers

Travel smart. Stay legal. Stay safe.®

From local laws to medical guides we've got you covered world wide in one digital platform.

Travel Safe Anywhere
3 MONTHS FREE TRIAL

SCAN QR code
for more info

PREFACE

My introduction to the justice system came when I was only 10 years old. My 15-year-old brother was murdered with a butcher knife by a 19-year-old in a simple argument over a torn shirt. I was devastated by his death and sought retribution for his fate that never came. The woman was initially charged with second-degree murder, but after plea negotiations, she was convicted of manslaughter and sentenced to only five years in a youthful offender school and ordered to undergo psychiatric care. That was it. Nothing more. The judicial system had run its course.

My family knew nothing about the justice system, and we did not have the tools to advocate for ourselves. No one provided us with a written source to reference for guidance through this process. There was no easily accessible, easy to understand, definitive source to use to educate ourselves about the legal system that we suddenly and unexpectedly found ourselves immersed in after being victimized by such a violent criminal act.

As I got older, finished college, law school, and ultimately started practicing law, it became clear to me that most people are not knowledgeable about the law or how the judicial process works. If most people are uninformed about the law and legal process here in the United States, how would they fare when in other countries? I realized that tourists and businesspeople who travel internationally needed access to information on how to navigate the legal system in other countries!

For many years, there has been considerable media attention focused on international travelers experiencing legal difficulties while traveling abroad. Most of these news stories gained attention in the United States and abroad because they involved American citizens facing punishment that was considered "unconventional" and "harsh" by United States' legal standards. I recall a news story in 1994 regarding Michael Fay, a young American male, who had broken the law in Singapore. He was convicted and sentenced to be caned and/or whipped publicly. While the United States government weighed in on the inappropriate and cruel nature of the punishment, the young American was beaten because he had been convicted under Singapore law.

In recent years, international news has highlighted stories of foreign travelers encountering legal issues in countries outside their own. Amanda Knox, an American woman, was accused of murdering her roommate in Italy in 2007 and spent almost four years in an Italian prison before being definitively acquitted by the Supreme Court of Cassatio. Kenneth Bae, an American citizen, was arrested in North Korea in 2012 and was convicted for hostile acts against the communist country. He was sentenced to 15 years hard labor but was released in 2014 after efforts by the U.S. State Department. More recently, United States Basketball Star, Brittany Griner, was arrested in February 2022 at a Moscow airport on drug-related charges and detained for nearly 10 months, spending much of that time in prison. Her plight unfolded at the same time Russia invaded Ukraine and further heightened tensions between Russia and the United States, ending only after she was freed in exchange for a notorious Russian arms dealer.

It was in 1994 that another personal tragic event occurred that finally inspired me to write this series of books. A dear friend and a client of mine was brutally murdered while on his second honeymoon in Jamaica. News of his murder shocked me and our local community. The legal hurdles his family had to overcome to see that justice was properly dispensed far away from home, in another country, with an entirely different set of criminal procedural rules and laws, was difficult to navigate.

As I was my friend's attorney at the time of his death, his family asked that I act as their "legal liaison" to the Jamaican Prosecutor's Office and to the Jamaican Police Department. I participated in multiple police interviews with my client's widow, since she was the primary witness to his murder. As a former prosecuting attorney, I was also allowed by the Court, as a professional courtesy, to sit at the prosecutor's table to consult with the prosecuting attorney during trial. What I witnessed firsthand during the Jamaican trial process was so compelling that it motivated me to seriously consider educating others on what to expect and how to behave appropriately when dealing with legal issues while traveling abroad.

One of the realities in life is that, regardless of what country you are in, it is never a pleasant experience to run afoul of the law and be forced to accept that someone else will be making a decision about your pecuniary, proprietary, or penal interests (your money, your property, or your freedom).

It is important to know what the laws are, how they apply to you, and how to navigate the legal system if you are charged with a crime. It is also very helpful to know what resources are available to you if you are the victim of a criminal act. At the end of the day, an "ounce of prevention is worth a pound of cure," so the more knowledge you have, the more ammunition you possess, and the more likely you will have a positive outcome.

If you are traveling to Italy, the first thing you should pack is a copy of this book! The helpful information and tips contained in this volume will provide a great starting point for knowing what to do (and not to do!), when you arrive at your destination and will help ensure you have a wonderful vacation or business trip unmarred by tangles with the law.

TABLE OF CONTENTS

INTRODUCTION

- About This Book
- Hypotheticals
- How This Book is Organized
- Icons Used Throughout This Book
- Where to Go From Here

INTRODUCTION

As a practicing attorney for over 34 years, I have encountered numerous clients who travel often but are unaware of the laws of the land they are traveling to.

Therefore, many years ago, I decided to write a series of books that would explain the laws of specific countries. My goal was to explain the laws that could impact travelers in a clear and simple way, avoiding the complex legal jargon that can be difficult to understand, even for experienced attorneys.

About This Book

The purpose of this book is straightforward: to offer travelers a clear, easy-to-read guide that provides a basic overview of the laws in the country they are about to visit. It is not intended to educate you on ALL of the laws in a given country. The goal is to provide you with the details of the most common legal and safety issues faced by tourists and business travelers.

I have also provided context with background information on places not to visit, statistics on the country, and prevention measures to safeguard your legal and physical safety. Knowledge is a powerful thing and knowing how to stay out of trouble (or how to get out of it!) is important for everyone who travels. This *Law of The Land/Italy* book simply helps you become more informed about your legal rights, responsibilities, and obligations in a wide range of subject areas.

Last, but not least, this book does NOT purport to offer legal advice. It does, however, provide the information you need to stay safe, follow the law, and navigate around legal difficulties. However, if you encounter a legal issue, the information in this book will serve as a starting point to help you address the problem and seek legal assistance if necessary.

Hypotheticals Used Throughout This Book

From time to time throughout this book, I will explain the law to readers by using hypothetical scenarios. These hypotheticals will be marked by an icon that will be explained in further detail as you read on.

How This Book is Organized

CHAPTER 1: **About Italy.** This chapter will provide you with a brief overview of Italy and its history. It also addresses Visa requirements, monetary advice, and the best times to visit.

CHAPTER 2: **Customs.** This chapter will provide information on what to expect when entering Italy. It will also explain what restricted and prohibited items are when entering Italy along with customs regulations.

CHAPTER 3: **Crime in Italy.** This chapter provides an overview of the history of crime in Italy and steps Italian officials have taken to curb the high rate of crime.

CHAPTER 4: **Criminal Law Violations.** This chapter will provide information on drug offenses, penalties, real life events, and answer some general interest questions.

CHAPTER 5: **Alcohol-Related Offenses.** This chapter will provide key points regarding the sale, consumption, and regulations of alcohol use in Italy.

CHAPTER 6: **Firearm & Ammunition Offenses.** This chapter will provide key points regarding the possession of firearms and ammunition in Italy.

CHAPTER 7: **Prostitution.** This chapter provides an overview of the history of prostitution in Italy, laws and penalties, prostitution practices, sex trafficking, sex tourism, health in Italy, tips to avoid being hassled, a Law of the Land Hypothetical, and the current situation on prostitution in Italy.

CHAPTER 8: **LGBTQ.** This chapter will provide information regarding the acceptance of LGBTQ people in Italy and the laws surrounding homosexuality.

CHAPTER 9: **Sexually Motivated/Violent Crimes.** This chapter will provide an overview of sexually-related crimes in Italy.

CHAPTER 10: **Arrested in Italy.** This chapter will provide information on what to do if you are arrested in Italy.

CHAPTER 11: **Jails vs. Prisons: Conditions & Culture.** This chapter will provide information on the conditions and culture of Italian jails and prisons.

CHAPTER 12: **Helping a Friend or Relative Imprisoned in Italy.** This chapter will provide information on how you can assist a friend or relative imprisoned in Italy.

CHAPTER 13: **The Administration of Justice.** This chapter will provide information on Italy's judicial system.

CHAPTER 14: **Crime Victim Assistance.** This chapter will provide information on crime victim assistance along with providing safety tips.

CHAPTER 15: **Police.** This chapter will provide information on the Italian Police and how to report a crime.

CHAPTER 16: **How to Get Legal Help in Italy.** This chapter will provide information on how to obtain legal assistance for travelers to Italy.

CHAPTER 17: **Medical Facilities & Hospitals.** This chapter will provide information about how to obtain medical care while visiting Italy.

CHAPTER 18: **Driving in Italy.** This chapter will provide information on driving in Italy, traffic rules, and road safety tips.

CHAPTER 19: **Nude Beaches & Clothing-Optional Resorts.** This chapter will provide an overview of nude beaches, and the legality and safety of visiting nude beaches in Italy.

CHAPTER 20: **Unusual Laws.** This chapter will provide information on some unusual laws in Italy, and associated penalties and fines.

CHAPTER 21: **Traveling Safely.** This chapter will provide information on women traveling alone, crime prevention for families, safety notes for all travelers, and overall advice.

CHAPTER 22: **Tourist Taxation.** This chapter will provide information on taxes that tourists are required to pay in Italy.

CHAPTER 23: **Long-Term Stays.** This chapter will provide an overview of the consequences for overstaying your visit to Italy.

CHAPTER 24: **Civil Litigation.** This chapter will provide information about the civil litigation process in Italy.

CHAPTER 25: **Other Things to Know.** This chapter will provide information on the harassment of tourists, travel and safety, and other practical tips.

CHAPTER 26: **Quick Reference Guide.** This chapter is a quick way to get information. It is a condensed version of the chapters in this book.

Emergency/Important Contact Numbers in Italy

Useful Italian Phrases

Glossary

Icons Used in this Book

What do those pictures throughout the book mean? See below:

 **WARNING**: This icon flags information about things you should **avoid** while visiting Italy. Heed the advice next to this icon to avoid legal perils.

 **REMEMBER**: This icon flags noteworthy information that you **shouldn't forget**.

 **HELPFUL TIPS**: This icon flags information that will help you when entering Italy, relates to a legal situation, or refers to resources available while visiting Italy.

 **TECHNICAL INFORMATION**: This icon flags technical aspects of the law. If you are faced with a legal problem, and you want to learn more about the law involved, this information can be helpful.

 **ADDITIONAL INFORMATION**: This icon points to the location of additional information available on the internet.

 **HYPOTHETICAL**: This icon points to hypothetical scenarios to illustrate possible legal problems and the outcome.

 **QUESTIONS**: This icon points to questions and answers throughout the book.

 **TRUE STORY**: This icon points to true events throughout the book.

Where to Go From Here

If you have a specific question about the law in Italy as it relates to a specific area, just turn to the chapter that addresses that issue or turn to the *Quick Reference Guide.*

You can also read the book from cover to cover to obtain a more comprehensive understanding of the Italian laws, and resources available should you find yourself in a legal predicament while visiting.

 **Disclaimer:** While the recommendations in this book primarily address U.S. citizens, the information is relevant and applicable to citizens of any country.

ABOUT ITALY

IN THIS CHAPTER

- Overview of Italy
- Visa Requirements
- ETIAS Requirements
- Monetary Advice
- General Questions
- Best Time to Visit

ABOUT ITALY

Overview of Italy

The Italian Republic, or Italy, is a country in the south of Europe, consisting mainly of a boot-shaped peninsula, together with two large islands in the Mediterranean Sea: Sicily and Sardinia. To the north, it is bound by the Alps, where it borders France, Switzerland, Austria, and Slovenia.

The country's main economic sectors are tourism, fashion, engineering, chemicals, motor vehicles, and food. Italy's northern regions are, per capita, amongst the richest in Europe.

The center of the vast Roman Empire, which left a huge archaeological, cultural and literary heritage, the Italian peninsula, saw the birth of medieval humanism and the Renaissance. This further helped to shape European political thought, philosophy, and art, via figures like Machiavelli, Dante, Leonardo da Vinci, and Galileo.

The list of famous Italian artists is long and includes Giotto, Botticelli, Leonardo, Michelangelo, Tintoretto, and Caravaggio. The country has also produced opera composers such as Verdi and Puccini, and film-maker Federico Fellini.

Italian cuisine is one of the most refined and varied in Europe, from the piquant flavors of Naples and Calabria, to the pesto dishes of Liguria, and the cheese and risotto dishes of the Italian Alps.[1]

Quick facts about Italy:

- **Capital:** Rome
- **Geographical size:** 302,073 km² (187,699.46 miles²)
- **Official Language:** Italian
- **Political system:** parliamentary republic
- **Currency:** Euro

 **Visa Requirements**

PASSPORT VALIDITY: Six months validity recommended, at least 3 months validity beyond your planned date of departure from the Schengen (comprised of European countries that have abolished internal border controls for free movement).

BLANK PASSPORT PAGES: Two pages required for entry stamp.

TOURIST VISA REQUIREMENTS: Not required for stays under 90 days.

---

1   https://www.eubusiness.com/euro/italy-and-the-euro/

ETIAS Requirements

Beginning in 2025, citizens of eligible countries need to apply for the ETIAS Italy before traveling to the country. The ETIAS (European Travel Information and Authorization System) will be introduced by the European Union for all Schengen area member countries.

The ETIAS for Italy will require previously visa-exempt citizens to complete an online ETIAS Italy application prior to their trip. Eligible travelers can obtain their ETIAS Italy by providing personal and passport details and answering a series of security questions. ETIAS will allow for improved border control within the Schengen area.

US citizens are currently exempt from obtaining a visa to Italy. All American travelers who wish to visit Italy in the future will be required to apply for the travel authorization and meet the ETIAS Italy requirements:

- A valid passport
- A debit or credit card
- An email address[2]

VACCINATIONS: None.

CURRENCY RESTRICTIONS FOR ENTRY: €10,000 (US$10,295.48) or equivalent.

CURRENCY RESTRICTIONS FOR EXIT: €10,000 (US$10,295.48) or equivalent.[3]

---

2 https://www.etiasitaly.com/requirements/united-states

3 https://travel.state.gov/content/travel/en/international-travel/International-Travel-Country-Information-Pages/Italy.html

Monetary Advice

First, understand that Italy is a very cash-oriented society, so make sure you always have some cash in your wallet. Businesses must accept credit or debit cards by law now and an increasing number of Italians are using plastic more than cash to make their daily purchases. However, to buy coffee, gelato, or a slice of pizza, most shops still prefer cash. You'll also need cash to shop at most outdoor food market stands, take a city taxi or buy a bus ticket, leave a tip (Italian credit card machines do not have a tip prompt since tipping is not mandatory in Italy), and pay the city tourist tax at many hotels.

On the other hand, don't carry too much cash on you either—flashing a wad of bills is a bad idea for obvious reasons. Almost all major attractions, hotels, B&Bs, restaurants, and shops accept credit and debit cards and anti-laundering laws make it illegal to pay more than €4,999 (US$5,266.95) in cash. In addition, many tour companies, guides, and drivers either accept credit cards or can arrange payment via platforms like *PayPal* or *SumUp* that allow customers to pay with plastic (generally, for a small service fee). While *Venmo* cannot be used in Italy, other payment apps like *ApplePay*, *GooglePay*, and *PayPal* can be.[4]

---

4   https://italybeyondtheobvious.com/a-money-strategy-for-your-italy-trip/

 **General Questions**

1. ***Where can you convert your currency into euros?*** You can convert your currency at the airport and in large train stations, and banks and exchange agencies, where you can withdraw cash or use related services.

   Banks (with 24/7 ATMs) are spread across Italy, where you can exchange/buy traveler's checks (in dollars or euros).

   The denominations of coins and banknotes are as follows:

   > Coin denominations: 1 cent, 2 cents, 5 cents, 10 cents, 20 cents, 50 cents, 1 euro, 2 euro.

   > Banknote denominations: 5 euro, 10 euro, 20 euro, 50 euro, 100 euro, 200 euro.

2. ***Which electronic payment systems are available?*** In addition to cash, you can pay for your purchases using the most popular credit cards. In larger tourist centers, it is also possible to pay using your smartphone via various dedicated apps.

   Currently, the main active electronic payment systems include:

   > Visa

   > MasterCard/Cirrus/Maestro

   > American Express

   > Bancomat

   > Postamat

   > PagoBancomat

3. ***Tipping in Italy: yes or no?*** Tipping in Italy is not compulsory, and there are no established rules, but it is customary to leave close to 10% of the bill when the customer is satisfied with the service.

4. ***Receipts and bills are obligatory.*** For any goods/services you decide to purchase in Italy, remember to ask for (and keep) the receipt or bill when you pay; this will allow you to justify your possession of goods and not incur fines in the event you are stopped and checked. In Italy, all official commercial businesses are under obligation to issue a payment slip, and every citizen must receive one after every purchase in accordance with the law. When purchasing products, it also allows you to make use of a guarantee or to make a return.

5. ***Haggling and discounts.*** In Italy, as a general rule, the prices of goods and services are those displayed or indicated in price lists; it is not customary to haggle over the price when purchasing an item.

   However, there are fairs and markets where it is possible to negotiate the price. In early July and after the Christmas holidays, Italian shops have sales, offering large discounts on products. The exact dates of the sales vary from region to region.[5]

Best Time to Visit

There's no wrong answer; it depends on what you want to discover.

Peak Season (June - August)

This is the busiest time to travel in Italy, with the largest crowds and the highest prices. The weather is generally warm and sunny, making it an excellent time for outdoor activities and beach trips. Also, many outdoor events and festivals occur during the summer in Italy.

---

5   https://www.italia.it/en/italy/practical-information/
    money-payments-and-tipping-in-italy

Shoulder Season (April - May, September - October):

The shoulder seasons offer a good balance between good weather, smaller crowds, and lower prices. It's a good time to explore Italy's museums, galleries, and churches. April and May are particularly nice for outdoor activities and sightseeing.

Off-Season (November - March)

This is the quietest time to travel in Italy, with the least amount of visitors and the lowest prices. The weather can be cold and rainy, but winter sports are popular in the mountains. Many attractions, shops, and restaurants may have reduced hours or be closed during the off-season, so checking before traveling is recommended.

CUSTOMS

CUSTOMS

Overview[6]

Customs is a longstanding institution that continually adapts to new challenges. In the European Union, customs policy is no longer solely managed by national authorities but is pursued through collective efforts across member states. Key objectives include improving the efficiency and harmonization of customs duties, ensuring the security and environmental compliance of goods, combating product counterfeiting (a significant issue in Italy), and tackling the trafficking of protected species and illegal substances.

Products and Consumer Goods

As of January 1, 1993, EUMS (European Union Member States) represent a free trade area for free circulation of people, goods and capitals. Hence, passengers moving within the European Union are allowed to carry goods purchased in any EU country without limitation and without having to fulfil customs formalities.

---

6   https://www.adm.gov.it/portale/docu-
     ments/20182/909438/Carta_viaggiatore_EN_20240911-r.
     pdf/98376006-a936-9315-126e-1e8544b28e4f?t=1726049807006

The only exceptions are certain categories of products, such as manufactured tobacco, alcohol, and alcoholic beverages, for which approximate thresholds are indicated below, referring to purchases by private persons.

Manufactured Tobacco:

- **Cigarettes:** 800 pieces
- **Cigarillos (max 3g each):** 400 pieces
- **Cigars:** 200 pieces
- **Smoking tobacco:** 1 kg (2.20 lbs)

Alcohol and Alcoholic Beverages:

- **Alcohol and beverages with an alcohol content over 22%:** 10 liters (2.64 gallons)
- **Alcohol and beverages with an alcohol content under 22%:** 20 liters (5.28 gallons)
- **Wine (including up to 60 liters of sparkling wine):** 90 liters (23.77 gallons)
- **Beer:** 110 liters (29.05 gallons)

Currency[7]

The transport of cash or other securities is allowed for amounts lower than €10,000 (US$10,536). For amounts equal to or exceeding €10,000 (US$10,536), a form must be filled out, signed, and lodged at the customs office upon arrival into, or upon departure, from Italy. The rule applies to movements from and to non-E.U. countries.

Failing to declare cash when required violates monetary regulations and may result in the following penalties:

---

7   https://wise.com/gb/blog/taking-cash-in-or-out-of-italy

- For cash amounts **equal to or less than** €**10,000** (**US$10,536**), administrative seizure of up to 30% of the excess amount, plus a fine ranging from 10% to 30% of the excess.

- For cash amounts **exceeding** €**10,000** (**US$10,536**), administrative seizure of up to 50% of the excess amount, plus a fine ranging from 30% to 50% of the excess.

 The forms for submitting the declaration can be accessed on the Agency's website at: **www.agenziadoganemonopoli.gov.it**.

Export

There are no restrictions on the value and quantity of exported products carried by travelers leaving Italy for another non-E.U. country. However, there may be restrictions set forth by destination countries. Therefore, it is recommended to contact the Foreign Service of your destination country before departure.

VAT Information

Value Added Tax (VAT) is a sales tax applied at each stage of the production and distribution process, with the final cost passed on to the consumer. The applicable VAT rate will be included in the price of the goods you buy. As a visitor to the EU, if you're returning home or traveling to another non-EU country, you may be eligible to purchase goods without VAT in designated stores.

The standard VAT rate in Italy is 22%. Italy will reimburse between 13% and 15% of the amount you spend during your trip on products subject to standard VAT rates. The minimum purchase threshold is €154.95.[8]

---

8   https://wise.com/gb/vat/italy

EU non-resident travelers may be granted a VAT (value added tax) refund or relief for goods purchased in Italy, provided that:

- the overall value of the purchased goods exceeds 154.94 € (US$170.45) (VAT included);
- the goods are intended for personal or family use and are carried in personal luggage;
- the purchase is certified by an invoice containing the description of goods, the personal data of the traveler, and the details of his/her passport or of any equivalent document;
- the goods leave the EU territory within three months, starting from the end of the month the product was purchased;
- the goods and the relevant invoice are shown at the customs exit from the EU territory for the ENDORSEMENT proving that the goods have effectively left the Community territory;
- the invoice thus endorsed is returned to the Italian seller within four months as of the end of the month the goods were purchased.

For a VAT refund or relief, the purchased goods must always be shown at the customs office.

This benefit may be also granted for goods not brought outside of the E.U. territory in the personal luggage of travelers, but which are forwarded to the foreign residence of the owner as "not accompanied" luggage.

In this case, the goods are shipped to their destination by airline and are subject to an air-freight agreement becoming effective as of the issuance of the airway bill (AWB) by the air carrier.

Other Traveling Considerations

Animals

Pets are allowed to travel across national boundaries, if they are more than three months of age, except where otherwise provided for by the competent authority.

If a passenger is bringing pets into Italy (no more than five), a health certificate issued by the appropriate health authorities in the country of origin must be presented. Such a certificate should contain detailed information about the animal and the owner, certifying the good health of the animal and valid rabies vaccination. For select third world countries, the certificate must also indicate the titration (concentration) of antibodies against rabies, carried out at least three months before leaving.

If the animal does not meet the requirements, the competent authority will decide whether the animal must be sent back to its country of origin or be placed in quarantine.

Medicines

Current regulations don't have special rules for importing medicines carried by passengers, except for drugs, psychotropic substances, and doping agents. However, if a passenger is carrying more than a 30-day supply for personal use, Health and Customs authorities typically request a medical prescription showing the dosage details.

 **Weapons**

Under public security regulations, the importation of firearms, knives, or other weapons is prohibited unless accompanied by a valid authorization from the competent authorities.

Flight Luggage Control

Customs and security checks are carried out in the departure country, even if the flight has a layover in an EU country before reaching a non-EU destination. If passengers transfer to another aircraft before leaving the EU, hand luggage will be inspected at the transit airport.

Upon arrival in the EU, customs checks take place in the destination country. If passengers need to change flights to reach another EU country, checked luggage is inspected at the last arrival airport, while hand luggage is checked at the first EU airport where duties are paid on goods purchased that exceed the exemption limit.

CRIME IN ITALY

CRIME IN ITALY

Overview

Some of this information may seem overwhelming, but the important thing to remember is to stay safe and be mindful and vigilant of any legitimate threat of crime. This chapter will help guide you through a safe stay in Italy.

In recent years, Italy has experienced fluctuating crime rates, with some categories seeing a decline while others have risen. Between 2011 and 2020, the homicide rate in Italy dropped significantly, from 555 to 278, reflecting a general decrease in violent crime.[9] However, in 2023, the overall crime rate increased by 3.8% compared to the previous year, with specific crimes like homicide and assault on the rise. In particular, homicides in 2023 reached 334, marking a 3.7% increase from 2022. This uptick in violent crimes is partly linked to issues such as domestic violence, with women disproportionately affected, as 117 of the homicide victims were female.[10]

Notwithstanding, you should exercise extra caution at night, especially at train stations, airports, nightclubs, bars, and outdoor cafes. If you are drinking heavily, your ability to judge situations and make decisions may be impaired, making you a target for crime. Young drinkers are particularly vulnerable to robbery and physical and sexual assault.

---

9   https://www.statista.com/topics/4051/crime-in-italy/

10   https://www.agenzianova.com/en/news/omicidi-in-italia-nel-2023-sono-334-aumentano-le-vittime-di-sesso-maschile

Petty crimes like pickpocketing, theft from parked cars, and purse snatching are widespread, particularly in large cities and crowded tourist areas. The most common thefts occur at major railway stations like Rome's Termini, Milan's Centrale, Florence's Santa Maria Novella, and Naples' Centrale at Piazza Garibaldi, as well as in busy public transportation settings like buses and trains.

Milan's Malpensa Airport and Internet cafes in major cities are also frequent targets for thieves. Criminals often work in pairs or groups, using distraction tactics to steal from unsuspecting tourists. For example, one thief may spill something on a victim to draw their attention, while another steals their belongings. Thieves on motor scooters are also a threat, snatching bags from people's arms as they ride by. In some cases, criminals use sharp blades to slit purses or bags to steal valuables without the victim noticing.

In more dangerous incidents, criminals have been known to drug tourists by offering them drinks laced with sleeping drugs. Once the victim falls asleep, the thieves steal their belongings, and some cases have even involved sexual assault or hospitalization. This type of crime has led to serious injury and, in rare instances, even death. Tourists are advised to remain vigilant and protective of their belongings in these high-risk environments.

Thieves have been known to impersonate police officers in order to steal from travelers. They may show you a plastic badge with the words "police" or "international police" and, speaking in fluent English, ask to see your ID and money. Travelers should be aware that real police officers typically exit their vehicles when interacting with the public. Additionally, plainclothes officers usually do not stop vehicles without a marked police car present. If you find yourself in this situation, ask to see the officer's identification before handing over your wallet, as impersonators often don't carry fake IDs. Always report thefts or suspicious activity to genuine police authorities immediately.

 Stay vigilant for the risk of carjackings and thefts while wait-ing in traffic, which has been a particular problem in Catania, Sicily. Use extreme caution while driving at night on high-ways, when thieves are more likely to strike. U.S. citizens have reported break-ins of their rental cars during stops at highway service areas; thieves smash car windows and steal everything inside. The theft of small items such as radios, luggage, cameras, briefcases, and even cigarettes from parked cars is prevalent. Vehicles parked near beaches during the summer can be broken into and robbed of valuables. Lock car doors whenever you park and do not leave possessions in your car in plain view.

Organized criminal groups operate throughout Italy but are more wide-spread in the south. They occasionally resort to violence to intimidate their victims or settle disputes among each other. Though the activities of such groups are not generally targeted at tourists, visitors should be aware as innocent bystanders could be injured.

 Don't buy counterfeit or pirated goods, even if they are widely available. Not only are the bootlegs illegal to bring back into the United States, but if you purchase them, you may also be breaking a local law.

According to Italian law, anyone caught buying counterfeit goods is subject to a fine of at least €1,000 (US$1,053.60). It is true that po-lice in major Italian cities enforce this law to varying degrees, never-theless, it is advisable to purchase products only from stores and other licensed retailers to avoid unknowingly buying counterfeit and illegal merchandise.[11]

---

11 https://www.countryreports.org/country/Italy/crimes.htm#:~:text=Ita-ly%20has%20a%20moderate%20rate,you%20a%20target%20for%20 crime.

 **Quick Safety Tips**

1. **Keep away from protests** – they can occur without any warning in the cities, and they're not fun to get caught up in.

2. **Be careful of public transport, big stations, and airports** – conducive to high levels of petty theft and muggings .

3. **Watch your belongings in busy tourist areas** – more tourists = more targets for pickpockets. Make sure that you wear a money belt to mitigate the risk of theft.

4. **Try to dress like a local** – in cities, tourists tend to dress well. Sportswear and flashy designer clothes won't blend in. Opt for chic, simple, and well-groomed outfits to fit in.

5. **Keep a tight hold on your bag in cafes** – leaving it on a chair, hanging it, or placing it on the floor can be risky. In a busy city, it could disappear in an instant.

6. **Leave valuables in your hotel safe** – if not, leave them hidden in your room and purchase a padlock to keep them safe.

7. **Use pedestrian crossings** – be careful of speedy vehicles, especially in big cities.

8. **Carry ID on you at all times** – it's the law. You should comply with the police if asked to produce your ID.

9. **Beware of beggars** – in large cities, they can get aggressive and often they're part of organized groups.

10. **Keep vigilant** – distraction tactics are common in Italian cities. These are often just schemes to steal from you. Be cautious and don't fall for anything that seems suspicious.

CRIMINAL LAW VIOLATIONS

CRIMINAL LAW VIOLATIONS

Marijuana Laws And Penalties

The recreational use of cannabis is **illegal** in Italy. However, small quantities of cannabis (up to 1.5 grams) for personal use, as well as "cannabis light" (containing less than 0.5% THC), are decriminalized under Italian law.

People who possess more than 1.5 grams of cannabis in Italy are subject to fines or the suspension of personal documents like driver's licenses and passports.

Delta 8, CBD, and CBG

Delta 8 THC is also **illegal** in Italy. Italian law does not permit the sale or possession of Delta 8.

Cannabis products with a THC content of 0.2% or less can be bought in stores all over Italy, but only from licensed suppliers. Private individuals should never try to cross international borders with their own product, even if it complies with the possession and sale law within the country.

CBD is **legal** in Italy as a result of a combination of both EU and domestic law. Following applicable EU guidelines, CBD products entering Italy must contain less than 0.3% THC and meet any other general import requirements. Italy is considered a CBD-friendly country with sales massively increasing through both brick-and-mortar and online platforms.

CBG, a lesser-known cannabinoid, has not been explicitly addressed by Italian law. As long as CBG products contain less than 0.3% THC, they are unlikely to face legal hurdles in Italy. With a strong interest in the benefits of THC and CBD, the Italian market is keen to explore new cannabinoids.

Other Drug Crimes and Penalties

Criminal law regarding the possession and distribution of drugs is governed by Presidential Decree No. 309/1990 (the Consolidated Law on Drugs, or *"Testo Unico stupefacenti"*), which outlines the regulations on drug possession, trafficking, and drug-related criminal organizations.

Drug dealing is considered a serious criminal offense and conspiracy to traffic drugs is punishable by law. While drug possession and use are subject to administrative penalties, they may result in sanctions such as a driving ban. Note that driving under the influence of narcotics is also a criminal offense.

Personal Possession vs. Drug Trafficking

In Italy, personal drug use isn't a criminal offense, but possession for personal use can result in administrative sanctions like suspension of driving or firearm privileges. First-time offenders typically receive a warning rather than sanctions, and they may be required to attend rehabilitation programs.

The distinction between personal possession and trafficking is based on factors like drug quantity, type, and packaging. Drug trafficking penalties vary by drug type:

- **Heavy drugs** (**e.g., heroin, cocaine**): 6-20 years in prison and fines from €25,822 (US$27,206.06) to €258,228 (US$272,069.02)
- **Light drugs** (**e.g., marijuana, hashish**): 2-6 years in prison and fines from €5,164 (US$5,440.79) to €77,468 (US$81,620.28)

Minor drug offenses carry sentences of 6 months to 4 years and fines from €1,032 (US$1,087.32) to €10,329 (US$10,882.63), regardless of drug type. Cooperation with authorities may reduce the sentence but doesn't prevent prosecution.

The most severe drug-related crime is **drug trafficking conspiracy**, where involvement in organizing or financing drug trade can lead to sentences of 20 years or more.

 **General Questions**

1. *What are the medical marijuana laws in Italy?* Medical marijuana is legal in Italy but strictly regulated. Since 2013, medical use of cannabis has been allowed in Italy with a doctor's prescription. Italy's healthcare system covers the cost of cannabis for serious health conditions like cancer and multiple sclerosis (MS). For other conditions, people need to pay for medical marijuana out of pocket.

   Medical cannabis supply in Italy is generally reserved for people who have tried conventional medical treatments that have failed.

2. *Is it legal to grow cannabis in Italy?* Small-scale cannabis cultivation of up to four plants is decriminalized in Italy. Trafficking and dealing cannabis, however, can lead to harsh criminal penalties of up to 10 years in prison.

3. ***Where is it safe to purchase cannabis in Italy?*** "Light" cannabis containing less than 0.5% THC content is legal to buy in Italy at any authorized retailer. The capital city of Rome is an especially popular destination for people purchasing "light" marijuana products.

4. ***Where is it safe to consume marijuana in Italy?*** If you are a tourist, you will be subject to the laws of Italy if you choose to consume cannabis. In addition to fines, people who consume cannabis illegally in Italy may have their driver's licenses revoked and passports confiscated. As such, it is safest to consume recreational cannabis that is less than 0.5% THC in the comfort of your own home or hotel room.

 **Law of the Land True Story**

In 2017, an Italian citizen was acquitted for growing marijuana on his balcony, as it was determined to be for medicinal use and not a criminal offense. The incident occurred near Turin, when a neighbor discovered 12 marijuana plants on the balcony. The man was initially placed under house arrest, but a Turin court later acquitted him, finding that the plants were cultivated for therapeutic purposes. The defendant acknowledged that the marijuana was not intended for sale, but solely for treating his health conditions. This case established a legal precedent for the self-cultivation of marijuana in Italy.

Similarly, in 2018, two young men in Italy were acquitted after being found with four marijuana plants and nine grams of cannabis at home. The court ruled that the plants did not meet the minimum size required for criminal prosecution and were intended solely for personal use. The defendants explained they grew the plants because they were tired of buying marijuana on the street, with all the associated risks, and had no intention or desire to sell the harvest.

 **Law of the Land Hypothetical**

HYPOTHETICAL: *Maria, a tourist visiting Italy, is walking through a park in Milan when a police officer stops her. The officer notices the smell of marijuana and asks if she is in possession of any drugs. Maria admits that she has a small amount of marijuana for personal use in her bag, which she brought with her from home.*

What are the legal consequences for Maria in this situation? Can she be arrested for having marijuana in Italy?

ANSWER: *In Italy, possessing small amounts of marijuana for personal use is decriminalized. If Maria is found with less than 1 gram, she would likely face a fine and have the marijuana confiscated, but not be arrested. However, smoking in public is illegal and could result in fines. Possessing larger quantities or evidence of distribution could lead to criminal charges. As a tourist, Maria should be aware that any drug-related offense could impact her future travel.*

CHAPTER 5

ALCOHOL-RELATED OFFENSES

ALCOHOL-RELATED OFFENSES

Legal Drinking Age

The legal drinking age in Italy is 18 and establishments can get fined for serving or selling alcohol to minors. It is a criminal offense to serve someone under 16 and can warrant a prison sentence of up to one year. On the other hand, serving someone over 16 is considered a minor offense resulting in a fine.

Drinking and Driving[12]

It is illegal to drive under the influence of alcohol in Italy. Penalties for driving under the influence (DUI) start at a blood alcohol level of 0.5 g/liter.

The police may establish the state of drunkenness by using an electronic breathalyzer, or alternatively, by taking a blood sample at the hospital, if the suspect is incapacitated or refuses the breath test.

---

12   https://www.hg.org/legal-articles/drink-driving-in-italy-44288

Penalties for drinking and driving

In Italy, penalties for drinking and driving depends on the blood alcohol concentration (BAC):

- **0 TO 0.5 G/L** *(Novice drivers under 21, within 3 years of getting a license):* Fine of €164 (US$172.79) – €663 (US$698.54), 5 points off the license. No criminal penalty.

- **0.5 TO 0.8 G/L** *(Mild Hypothesis):* Fine of €531 (US$559.46) – €2,125 (US$2,238.90), plus a 3–6 month license suspension. No criminal penalty.

- **0.8 TO 1.5 G/L** *(Medium Hypothesis):* Fine of €800 (US$800) – €3,200 (US$3,371.52), up to 6 months imprisonment.

- **ABOVE 1.5 G/L** *(Serious Hypothesis):* Fine of €1,500 (US$1,580) – €6,000 (US$6,321.60), 6 months to 1 year imprisonment. 1–2 year license suspension.

If the driver causes an accident, penalties are doubled, the vehicle may be impounded for 180 days. Driving between 10 pm and 7 am also increases penalties.

Additional penalties apply for bus or freight vehicle drivers, repeat offenders, or those involved in an accident with a BAC over 1.5 g/l or if they are under the influence of drugs.

A driver must be informed of their right to a lawyer prior to taking sobriety tests, or the test results may be invalid.

? General Questions

1. *I am only 18 years old. Will I get into trouble for possessing an open container of alcohol in public?* **No**. 18 is the legal drinking age in Italy. Italy has no open container laws, and a person may drink alcoholic beverages in public and not risk any legal repercussions.

2. *Can I drink in public places?* **Yes**. Public drinking is the custom in Italy. So yes, you can take your drink to go! However, your behavior has to stay in control.

Law of the Land True Story[13]

A court in Pordenone, northern Italy, sentenced American servicewoman, Julia Bravo, to a suspended prison term of two years and six months for causing a fatal road accident. In August 2022, Bravo, 21, struck and killed 15-year-old Giovanni Zanier while he was cycling on a path in Porcia, near the USAF Base in Aviano, where Bravo was stationed.

Although Bravo tested positive for alcohol after the incident, the court did not treat drunk driving as an aggravating factor since the alcohol test was conducted more than two hours after the crash, making it inadmissible as evidence of intoxication at the time of the accident.

---

13   https://www.stripes.com/branches/air_force/2024-03-19/julia-bravo-sentence-italy-13362589.html

FIREARM & AMMUNITION OFFENSES

FIREARM & AMMUNITION OFFENSES

Overview

Italians do not have a fundamental right to bear arms, and there are tough laws regulating both ownership and use of guns in the country.

Before buying a gun, you first need to get a gun-purchasing license *(Licenza di porto d'armi o Nulla osta)*, which is necessary even if you inherit or are gifted a weapon. To qualify, you must be over 18, provide a certificate from a shooting range confirming your ability to safely handle a firearm, have a clean criminal record, and declare that you do not have any mental health issues or drug addiction problems.

Once you possess a gun, it must be reported to the Interior Ministry within a 72-hour period by going to a police station and filing a declaration. Even with the purchasing license, there are limits to the number of weapons and ammunition you can possess. Guns cannot be transported outside the home loaded, unless you have a personal protection/concealed carry license, for which you must prove to have a valid reason.

 **Categories of Firearms Under Italian Law[14]**

In Italy, firearms are categorized into various classes based on their type, use, and potential impact on public safety. This classification system is crucial for enforcing appropriate regulations and restrictions for each category. The primary categories include:

- **Common firearms:** handguns, rifles, and shotguns typically used for sporting and hunting.
- **Defensive weapons:** firearms intended for personal protection.
- **Collectible firearms:** Older firearms that are considered collectibles due to their historical value and are usually not intended for use.
- **Automatic weapons:** Firearms capable of firing a succession of rounds with a single operation of the trigger. These are highly regulated and, in most cases, prohibited for civil use.

Understanding the category into which a firearm falls is the first step toward comprehending the associated legal obligations and permissions.

In addition, legal self-defense weapons include pepper spray and small knives with blades under 10 cm. Tasers and stun guns are illegal, as are firearms, which are heavily regulated. Concealed carry permits are rare, and open carry is generally reserved for law enforcement.

There are also limits on the types and quantities of firearms and ammunition that can be owned. For example, licensed individuals can keep 1,500 rounds of hunting ammunition but only 200 rounds of handgun ammunition.

---

14 https://www.vaia.com/en-us/explanations/italian/italian-social-issues/gun-control-italy/#:~:text=Modern%20Italian%20Firearms%20Regulation%20Explained,ammunition%20that%20can%20be%20owned.

It is illegal to carry weapons in public places, except for hunting, shooting sports, or personal defense. Automatic firearms, firearms disguised as other objects, and certain types of ammunition are also prohibited.

 ## Takeaways

- Gun control in Italy includes thorough background checks, licensing requirements, and regulations for firearm storage and transport to ensure public safety.

- Modern Italian firearms regulations entail a detailed system designed to ensure public safety with stringent controls on gun ownership and responsibilities.

- Categories of firearms under Italian law—common firearms, defensive weapons, collectible firearms, and automatic weapons. Each have specific regulations.

- The process of acquiring a gun in Italy involves obtaining a firearm license, completing a safety course, and obtaining medical certification to ensure responsible ownership.

 ## General Questions

1. *Can a tourist in Italy on vacation walk around freely armed with guns in Italian towns?* **No.** In Italy, gun ownership is strictly controlled. Firearms are prohibited without special written permission, and even with authorization, they can only be kept at home or used for specific activities like sports or hunting. Carrying a firearm in public is illegal.

2. *Can I fly with a firearm to Italy?* Theoretically, **yes**, with rigorous restrictions. All firearms and/or ammunition must be declared by the carrier and weapons must be unloaded. Firearms and/or ammunition may be admitted for transport as checked-in luggage, which cannot be accessed by passengers during the flight. Ammunition must not exceed 5 kilograms (33.06 lbs.) in gross weight, must be firmly secured, and the container must be clearly marked.[15]

Law of the Land Hypothetical

HYPOTHETICAL: *Kathy was enjoying a day of sightseeing in Rome when, unexpectedly, a robber approached her in a busy area. The situation quickly escalated as the thief attempted to steal her belongings. Kathy pulled out her pepper spray and sprayed the robber. Blinded and disoriented, he fled the scene in panic. Kathy immediately dialed the police to report the incident. Was she in any legal trouble for using pepper spray?*

ANSWER: **No!** *Under Italian law, Kathy would not face arrest for using the pepper spray. Pepper spray is legal in Italy for self-defense purposes, as long as the container is within the legal size limit. It can be used by individuals to protect themselves from immediate threats, such as the robbery Kathy faced. Therefore, her actions were fully justified, and she was not in violation of any laws.*

---

15 https://tinyurl.com/5x7hptz5

CHAPTER 7

PROSTITUTION

PROSTITUTION

Overview[16]

Sex work, or the sex trade, is a term used to refer to all aspects of work in the sex industry, primarily prostitution. This encompasses a range of activities such as escorting, prostitution, exotic dancing, pornography, camgirl/camboy work, phone sex work, and more.

It's important to note that there are many discussions and controversies regarding sex work, including issues related to legality, morality, personal autonomy, abuse, and exploitation. In some places, various forms of sex work are legal and regulated, while in others, they're illegal. Many sex workers' rights activists advocate for the decriminalization of sex work, allowing workers access to legal protections and safer working conditions.

Escorts

In Italy, being an escort or using escort services is legal, but the legal framework surrounding sex work is complex. While prostitution itself is not illegal, activities like pimping, human trafficking, and running brothels are prohibited. This creates a legal environment where sex workers can operate, but they lack the legal protections found in countries with

---

16   https://www.avvocatocivilistaroma.it/en/sex-work-in-italy/

regulated prostitution. As a result, Italian sex workers often face social stigma, violence, and fines for public order violations.

 ## The Merlin Law of 1958[17]

The Merlin Law (L75/1958), named after its author Lina Merlin, came into effect on September 20, 1958, and remains largely unchanged today. The law is a significant piece of legislation in Italy that regulates sex work by criminalizing certain activities, while decriminalizing prostitution itself.

The law criminalizes activities such as loitering, soliciting, and exploiting prostitution. It also prohibits prostitution in specific public places, including hotels, dance halls, and entertainment venues. However, prostitution itself is not a criminal act in Italy.

In addition, the law abolished the regulation of prostitution, closed brothels, and prohibited the registration of sex workers in public security records. It also ended mandatory health checks for women involved in prostitution and introduced the crime of "exploitation of prostitution," which targets those who profit from or coerce individuals into sex work.

Many Italian feminists view it as a foundational step in framing a human rights-based critique of commercial sexual exploitation. While the law aimed to reduce the exploitation and coercion of women in prostitution, it also closed legal brothels in Italy aiming to end the exploitation of women, some argue it inadvertently made sex workers more vulnerable.

Various activist groups in Italy are seeking to change laws regarding sex work, arguing that decriminalization and regulation can provide more security and dignity for the sex workers. However, these efforts are controversial and face significant opposition.

---

17 https://www.avvocatocivilistaroma.it/en/sex-work-in-italy/

Sex Workers' Rights in Italy

Sex workers have the right to safety and dignity, and as any other human being, they are entitled to all the protections derived from the constitution, international conventions, and laws.

Prostitution itself is not illegal in Italy, but many activities related to it are criminally punishable, such as exploitation, human trafficking, and facilitation of prostitution. This legal framework, often referred to as a "prohibitionist" model, allows a person to legally sell sexual services in Italy, but they cannot work in a brothel or have a pimp or manager.

When it comes to rights, sex workers in Italy find themselves in a complex situation. They don't have the right to standard occupational protections like workplace accident insurance, pensions, maternity, and sickness benefits, because their profession isn't recognized as "legitimate work." Additionally, they can't report workplace abuses without fearing fines or prosecution for related offenses, such as disturbing public peace.

Nevertheless, sex workers, like all citizens, are entitled to personal protection and safety. They have the right to refuse a client or service and to report acts of violence or crimes against them. However, due to social stigma and fear of discrimination or persecution, many sex workers may feel uncomfortable seeking help from law enforcement.

Several organizations and activist groups in Italy are working to change the law and achieve greater recognition and protection for sex workers, but progress is slow, and the issue is highly controversial. Many emphasize the importance of listening to the perspectives of sex workers themselves in these conversations since they are the ones directly affected by laws and policies related to their work. Their voices offer valuable insights into the real challenges they face, which might not be fully understood or represented by those who do not experience sex work firsthand.

Italian Laws on Prostitution

- **Selling sex:** Legal, however soliciting sex is not legal.

- **Buying sex:** Not criminalized by national law, but many local areas have by-laws that criminalize buying sex on the streets.

- **Organizing or managing:** Criminalized, including maintaining brothels, pimping, and human trafficking.

- **Working indoors:** Criminalized, but widely tolerated.

- **Sharing premises:** Illegal to share premises with another sex worker.

General Questions

1. *Do prostitutes have to pay taxes?* **Yes**, sex workers in Italy are required to pay taxes on income earned from their work, even if they do not have a business registration or a VAT number.

2. *Is there mandatory HIV/STI testing?* **No**. Prostitutes in Italy are not subject to mandatory health checks.

3. *Is there mandatory registration for sex workers?* **No**, there is no mandatory registration for sex workers in Italy. The Merlin Law abolished the requirement for sex workers to be registered in public security records, which had previously been part of the state's regulation of prostitution.

4. *Is prostitution legal in Italy?* **Yes**. Prostitution is legal in Italy. However, organized prostitution and brothels are not.

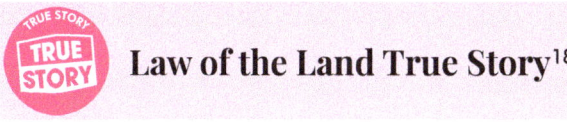

Law of the Land True Story[18]

Clients who don't pay prostitutes are guilty of rape, Italy's highest court ruled in 2012.

Italy's highest court, the Cassation Court, which sets legal precedents with its rulings, upheld a four-year rape conviction against a man from Liguria, who fled a hotel without paying for sex. The court stated that there was "no doubt" the man had abused the woman and was fully aware of his actions. The judges ruled that the encounter was not consensual because the sex act occurred "only in exchange for the fee owed." Diego S., 50, further aggravated his crime by persuading the hotel to deny his presence there, the court noted. He was ordered to pay €2,000 (US$2,097.40) to the sex worker.

18 https://www.ansa.it/web/notizie/rubriche/english/2010/03/03/visualizza_new.html_1709992053.html

CHAPTER 8
LGBTQ

LGBTQ

Overview[19]

Lesbian, gay, bisexual, transgender, and queer rights in Italy significantly advanced in the 21st century. Nonetheless, the LGBTQ population still faces various challenges despite increasingly liberal public opinion.

According to ILGA-Europe's 2021 report, LGBTQ rights in Italy fall short of the standards seen in some other Western European countries. Key issues include the lack of full recognition for same-sex marriage, the absence of nationwide anti-discrimination protections for goods and services, and the denial of full parental rights to same-sex couples, such as joint adoption and access to IVF (Invitro Fertilization). Italy and Japan are the only G7 nations where same-sex marriages are not permitted.[20]

Homosexual Activity and Same-Sex Marriage

Same-sex relationships are legal and generally accepted in Italy. Same-sex sexual activity has been legal since 1890.

19 https://www.equaldex.com/region/italy

20 https://en.wikipedia.org/wiki/LGBT_rights_in_Italy#:~:text=In%20 Italy%20both%20male%20and,sex%20couples%20as%20a%20family.

Since 2016, same-sex couples can enter civil unions, which grant many of the same rights as marriage. Public opinion is increasingly supportive, with 70.1% of Italians backing civil unions, 65.2% supporting same-sex marriage, and 51.4% in favor of same-sex adoption, according to a 2023 poll.[21]

Milan is considered Italy's gay capital, with an active LGBTQ+ scene. Other cities like Rome, Bologna, and Sicily are also known for being LGBTQ+ friendly. Italy's history, including the love story of Emperor Hadrian and Antinous, as well as Michelangelo's artistic inspiration, reflects a hidden gay culture.

However, there are still areas needing improvement. While there are anti-discrimination laws in employment, sexual orientation and gender identity are not fully protected in other areas of life. Civil unions do not grant same-sex couples joint adoption rights, although the Supreme Court has allowed stepchild adoption in some cases. Public perception of LGBTQ+ people in Italy is generally positive but lags behind many other EU countries.

Right To Change Legal Gender in Italy

In Italy, the right to change legal gender is **legal** but requires medical diagnosis. However, a Supreme Court ruling overturned the previous requirement for surgery to change legal gender. On February 15, 2023, a court in Trento ruled that transgender minors could have their legal gender changed on official documents, provided they have parental consent and have consulted with a psychologist.

---

21   https://en.wikipedia.org/wiki/LGBTQ_rights_in_Italy#:~:text=In%20
2023%2C%20a%20new%20poll%20showed%20a,also%20for%20
adoption%20by%20same%2Dsex%20couples%20(51.4%).

Gender-Affirming Care/Non-Binary Recognition in Italy

Gender-affirming care is legal in Italy. In 2003, the country adopted the ICD-10 classification, which includes diagnostic codes for transsexualism in both adults and children, allowing for the initiation of medical transition.

However, Italy does not yet officially recognize non-binary identities. That said, in a landmark ruling on March 7, 2022, an Italian court granted a non-binary person the legal recognition of their gender. This case remains the only instance of such recognition in the country.

LGBTQ Discrimination

LGBTQ+ discrimination is not legally allowed in Italy. Discrimination based on sexual orientation and gender identity is prohibited under Italian law.

In 2013, Italy passed a law that made it illegal to discriminate against individuals based on sexual orientation and gender identity in the workplace. However, while there are laws protecting against discrimination in employment, there is no comprehensive nationwide law that specifically protects LGBTQ+ people in all areas of life, such as access to goods and services, housing, or education.

LGBTQ+ discrimination in Italy can vary by region, with some areas offering stronger protections than others. Some cities like Milan, Bologna, and Rome have more inclusive policies and active support for LGBTQ+ individuals, while more conservative regions, particularly in the south, may have weaker protections and face challenges in addressing LGBTQ+ issues.

General Questions

1. *Is Italy LGBTQ+ friendly?* **Yes**. Italy is largely accepting and welcoming of those on the LGBTQ+ spectrum. Travelers visiting tourist-heavy areas such as Milan, Venice, Florence, and Rome should have no fear expressing themselves and enjoying a hassle-free holiday. [22]

2. *What cities in Italy are most gay friendly?* Rome, Catania, Bolgna, Florence, Milan, Naples, Padua, Gallipolio, and Pisa.[23]

Law of the Land True Story

A state prosecutor in northern Italy demanded the cancellation of 33 birth certificates of children born to lesbian couples dating back to 2017 after the government—a firm believer that children should be raised by heterosexual parents—began demanding that councils register only the biological parents.

Although a court in Padua rejected taking such action, the Ministry of the Interior has challenged the court's decision. Dismissal of so many LGBTQ+ cases as if they have no human rights often verge on the surreal, like the one where a child's birth certificate may all of a sudden be deemed invalid. The very existence of a child—including their right to be able to keep living with their non-biological mother in the event of their other mother dying—is treated as a matter of judgment, not as a basic human right.[24]

---

22 https://www.intrepidtravel.com/en/italy/is-italy-lgbtqia-friendly

23 https://www.visititaly.eu/places-and-tours/
the-5-most-lgbt-destinations-in-italy-what-they-are-and-why

24 https://www.theguardian.com/commentisfree/article/2024/jul/19/
italy-queer-rights-giorgia-meloni-lgbtq-community

CHAPTER 9

SEXUALLY MOTIVATED/ VIOLENT CRIMES

- Overview
- Sex Crimes And Penalties
- Reporting Sexual Assault in Italy
- General Questions
- Law of the Land True Story

SEXUALLY MOTIVATED/ VIOLENT CRIMES

Overview[25]

In the 2024 *Crime Index* published by *Sole 24 Ore*, the major tourist cities of Milan, Rome, and Florence are ranked among the most dangerous cities in Italy. The report shows that crime rates in Italy have increased for the first time since 2013, with a 3.8% rise compared to 2022, driven particularly by violent crimes such as homicides, assaults, injuries, and robberies. Milan, which has held the top spot for several years, reported the highest number of crimes in 2023, with over 7,000 reports per 100,000 inhabitants. The city saw a 4.9% increase in crime compared to the pre-pandemic period, with thefts and robberies at the forefront. It also ranked third for sexual violence and fifth for drug-related offenses.

Rome, while experiencing a rise in crimes (with a 16.7% increase from 2019 and 11% from 2022), saw the most notable uptick in thefts and street robberies, up 17% and 24% respectively. Florence, which has returned to the crime podium, experienced a dramatic 56% rise in street robberies compared to 2022, largely attributed to the flow of tourists. The report also notes that metropolitan cities and tourist destinations,

---

25 https://www.agenzianova.com/en/news/crime-in-italy-milan-rome-and-florence-at-the-top-of-the-ranking-of-the-sole-24-ore/

which attract millions of visitors annually, tend to have higher rates of predatory and violent crimes.

A significant new feature in the 2024 index is the increased impact of large metropolitan cities on overall crime rates in Italy. The 14 main metropolitan areas accounted for 30% of all crimes reported in 2023, with Milan and Rome alone making up 15% of this total. Other cities in the top 10 include Florence, Rimini, Turin, Bologna, Prato, Imperia, and Livorno, with Venice rising into the top 10, displacing Naples.

In contrast to the urban centers, provinces like Oristano, Potenza, and Treviso are among the safest in Italy, with crime rates significantly lower. These regions may benefit from stronger local control or a cultural "code of silence," though this could also reflect less effective state intervention.

Sex Crimes And Penalties

In Italy, the crime of sexual violence is categorized under "crimes against sexual freedom" or more broadly, "crimes against individual liberty," as defined in Article 609 of the Italian Penal Code.

Sexual violence, which is punishable by law, includes the following acts:

- **Sexual violence by coercion:** Forcing someone to engage in or endure sexual acts through physical violence, threats, or abuse of authority.
- **Sexual violence by exploitation of inferiority:** Coercing someone into sexual acts by taking advantage of their physical or mental incapacity at the time of the act.
- **Sexual violence by deception:** Inducing someone to engage in sexual acts through misleading them, such as impersonating another person.

The offense can be committed by anyone, including a spouse. The victim of sexual violence can be any person, regardless of gender or sexual orientation, including men, women, and individuals from the LGBTQ+ community.

 ## Reporting Sexual Assault in Italy

If you choose to report a sexual assault, it is important to keep in mind that the legal process is very slow. In Italy, the public prosecutor's office has six months to a year to carry out an investigation of a suspect. If an investigation turns out to be complex, the term for completing the investigation may be extended to between 18 months and two years. You can receive a medical examination without filing a report, if you wish. It is important to receive medical attention within 72 hours to receive the best care and collect the most evidence.

In certain instances of sexual violence, the police are required to initiate an investigation automatically, regardless of whether a complaint is filed by the victim. This typically occurs when the victim is under 18 years old, or when the physical injuries sustained are serious enough to require hospitalization for an extended period of time.

Sexual Assault Services

- **RAINN (Rape, Abuse & Incest National Network):** While RAINN primarily serves the U.S., they have resources and information that may be useful for Americans abroad. They offer a confidential 24/7 hotline at 1-800-656-HOPE, and their website has information on international resources.

- **The American Citizen Services (ACS) unit at U.S. embassies and consulates:** This service assists Americans abroad with various issues, including sexual assault. They can help with contacting local authorities, accessing medical care, and getting legal assistance.

- **Hospitals:**

  Florence: Studio Medico Associato
  Via Roma 4, 50123, Florence
  Tel: 055/475411

  Milan: Mangiagalli Hospital, Sexual Assault First Aid,
  c/o Clinica Mangiagalli, Via della Commenda, 12
  Tel (first aid): 02 55032489
  Email: svs@policlinico.mi.it

 **Legal Aspects of Reporting an Incident**

A case can take up to two years before it reaches trial. On average, trials last about two years, after which a verdict is delivered. The defendant automatically has the right to appeal, which typically leads to a second trial unless a plea agreement is reached. In some instances, the case may be appealed to the Supreme Court, where a final and enforceable ruling is made, potentially resulting in a third trial.

It is highly recommended to hire a local lawyer. Your lawyer will provide you with an address, required to receive any legal notifications, particularly if you do not reside in Italy. Your lawyer will represent you in Italy, so that you are not required to be present at every court session, though, you will need to appear in court for the first hearing.

In Italy, victims of rape and sexual assault are entitled to free legal aid. However, free legal aid is only implemented at the start of legal proceedings, which means that it does not cover preliminary actions provided by the lawyer. In some cases, lawyers will charge the client for services rendered before the case goes to court. This is something you should discuss with your lawyer prior to retaining their services.

 **General Questions**

1. ***What is the age of consent in Italy?*** In Italy, the age of consent is **14 years old**. Individuals who are 13 or younger are legally unable to consent to sexual activity, and engaging in such acts may lead to prosecution for statutory rape or its legal equivalent. Additionally, it is illegal to engage in sexual acts in the presence of a minor under 14, even if the minor does not actively participate.[26]

---

26 https://worldpopulationreview.com/country-rankings/
   age-of-consent-by-country

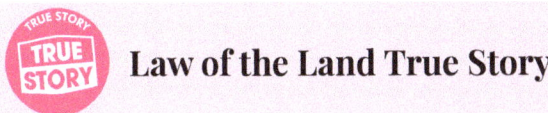 **Law of the Land True Story**

Shattered glass surrounds the abandoned swimming pool, along with dilapidated benches, broken tiles, and a single dirty mattress. Local police officers have identified the forsaken spot as one of the places where they say two young girls were repeatedly raped by a gang of their peers, all residents of the Italian town of Caivano, on the outskirts of Naples.

Though the rapes of the two girls, cousins just 10 and 12 years old, took place over many months, they seized national attention in 2023 after they were reported by the local news media, hurling the issue of violence against women and girls in Italy back into the spotlight.[27]

---

27 https://www.nytimes.com/2023/09/03/world/europe/italy-rape-women-violence.html

ARRESTED IN ITALY

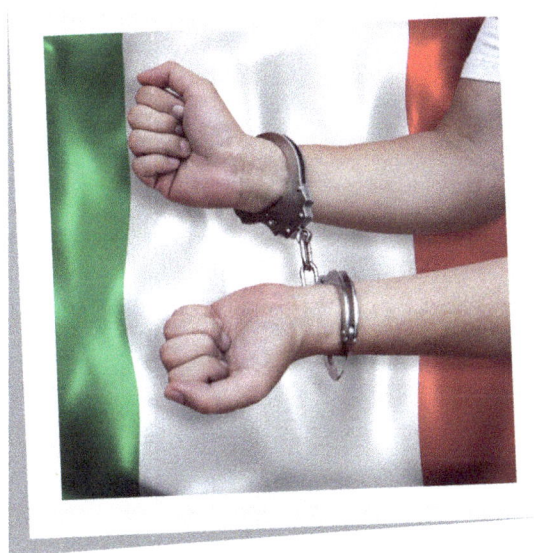

ARRESTED IN ITALY

Overview

When traveling in a foreign country, it's imperative to recognize that you are subject to the legal jurisdiction and regulations of that nation. These laws may significantly differ from those in your home country and might not offer the same legal protections you are accustomed to. It's crucial to bear in mind that penalties for violating foreign laws can be more severe than those for similar offenses in your home country, and ignorance of these laws is not typically accepted as a defense.

The consequences for breaking the law while abroad can be severe and may include expulsion, fines, arrest, or imprisonment. Even unintentional violations can lead to serious legal repercussions. It is essential for travelers to be aware of and adhere to the laws of the host country to avoid legal entanglements and ensure a safe and enjoyable experience.

Specifically, stringent penalties are often enforced for possession, use, or trafficking of illegal drugs in many countries. Convicted offenders can expect severe consequences, including lengthy jail sentences and hefty fines. The legal processes for foreigners in the event of an arrest abroad involve being charged or indicted, prosecuted, potentially convicted and sentenced, and, if applicable, going through an appeals process.

Navigating a foreign legal system can be complex, and individuals arrested abroad must be prepared to comply with the legal procedures of the host country. Seeking legal representation and understanding the local legal nuances are crucial steps for those facing legal issues in a foreign jurisdiction.

Awareness of and adherence to the laws of a foreign country are paramount when traveling. Understanding the potential consequences for legal violations and being prepared to navigate the legal system of the host country are essential aspects of responsible international travel.

Arrest Process

In Italy, when someone is arrested, the police must immediately inform the Public Prosecutor, the suspect's defense attorney, and their family. Within 48 hours, a judge (*Giudice delle Indagini Preliminari* or G.I.P.) must review the arrest to ensure its legality and decide whether to release the suspect or keep them in custody based on the evidence presented by the prosecutor. This validation hearing is essential to protect the suspect's right to legal representation and to confirm the arrest was lawful.

The arrest process begins with a preliminary investigation by the Public Prosecutor and Judiciary Police, who gather evidence after a crime is reported. Police can arrest a person if there is sufficient circumstantial evidence of guilt or if there is a risk the suspect may flee. Once arrested, the individual has the right to consult with a lawyer at any point, and if they cannot afford one, the court will appoint legal counsel. Pre-trial detention is possible but subject to strict limitations; a judge must assess whether it is necessary based on the specific circumstances of the case.[28]

Juvenile Criminal Responsibility

In Italy, criminal responsibility begins at age 14. Juveniles aged 14 to 18 can be charged with criminal offenses, if they are mentally capable of understanding their actions. For minors in this age group, the court assesses their mental capacity to determine culpability, and cases are

---

28 https://cild.eu/wp-content/uploads/2017/05/EN_KYR_
    VademecumPolice-4.pdf

handled by a specialized juvenile court. The Italian juvenile justice system emphasizes rehabilitation over punishment, prioritizing alternative measures such as probation, community service, and educational programs instead of incarceration whenever possible. **Children under 14 cannot be held criminally responsible under any circumstances.**[29]

Special Considerations for Non-Citizens

Non-citizens in Italy have the same rights as citizens within the criminal justice system, including the right to a fair trial, legal representation, and legal protections. However, language barriers and challenges accessing translation services can impact undocumented migrants' ability to fully participate in legal proceedings. While translation services are legally required for non-Italian speakers, issues with the quality and availability of these services persist. Non-citizens are entitled to legal aid, but their immigration status can influence how they are treated within the criminal justice system, particularly when deportation may be a potential consequence of a conviction.

Notify Your Home Country's Embassy

If you or a family member are arrested, local authorities must notify your country's embassy under the Vienna Convention. You may ask that local police contact your embassy on your behalf.

---

29 https://www.giustizia.it/giustizia/it/contentview.page?contentId=ART1123482&previsiousPage=mg_1_12_1#:~:text=Art.,%E2%80%9D%20Therefore%2C%20according%20to%20art

Rights of the Arrested Person

Under Italian law, an arrested person has the right to be informed of the charges against them, the right to remain silent, the right to immediate access to a lawyer (including a court-appointed one, if they cannot afford one), the right to contact a family member, and the right to an interpreter if they do not speak Italian. They should also be informed about their right to consular assistance, if they are a foreign citizen. An arrested person can be detained for a maximum of 24 hours before appearing before a judge.[30]

Getting Legal Assistance

Under the *Vienna Convention on Consular Relations* (April 24, 1963), when a foreign national is arrested in Italy, authorities are required to inform them of their right to request assistance from their consulate or embassy. **However, Italian authorities are not required to notify the consulate of an arrest *unless* the detainee requests it...so make sure you do!**

Typically, the consulate offers the following services:

- Prison visits by a consular officer.
- A list of local lawyers and their contact information.
- Communication with family (only with the prisoner's consent).
- Assistance with medical care and basic needs (when necessary and permitted by local regulations).

Foreign consulates do not participate in legal proceedings and are not responsible for covering legal fees. The level of consular assistance can vary based on the laws and services of the detainee's home country and its available resources. If you are a foreign national arrested in Italy, it is important to notify your embassy or consulate right away. For U.S.

---

30 https://cild.eu/wp-content/uploads/2017/05/EN_KYR_ VademecumPolice-4.pdf

citizens, you can use the American Citizens Services Contact Form to inform the U.S. Embassy or consulate. They can help contact family, friends, or employers (with consent), visit the detainee in jail, ensure appropriate medical care, explain the local legal system, and connect you with English-speaking attorneys. However, their assistance is limited—they cannot secure your release, provide legal advice, represent you in court, serve as interpreters or translators, or cover legal, medical, or other expenses.

Bail

In Italy, there is no bail system like in the United States. Instead, pre-trial detention is used in specific cases where there is a risk the accused may flee or interfere with the investigation. A judge can decide to detain the suspect until the trial, but this decision can be appealed to the *Corte di Libertà* (Court of Liberty).

Pre-trial detention in Italy is subject to strict criteria. A suspect can only be held if there is strong evidence suggesting they committed the crime and a risk that they might flee or obstruct justice. If a suspect is detained, they have the right to challenge the detention decision through an appeal to the Court of Liberty.

Foreign nationals facing pre-trial detention are subject to the same legal procedures as Italian citizens, but their immigration status can influence the decision. They may face stricter scrutiny regarding the risk of fleeing, especially if they lack legal residence or strong ties to Italy. Deportation risks may also affect detention decisions, as authorities may consider whether deportation is a possibility after a conviction.

Complaints Against Police

Italy's primary police force, the *Carabinieri*, is highly respected for its professionalism, effectiveness, and reputation for incorruptibility, earning it the nickname *La Benemerita* (The Meritorious) due to its trusted status among the Italian public. The Carabinieri are seen as a disciplined, military-style police force, known for their crucial role in combating organized crime, including the Mafia, and terrorism. They are often praised for their de-escalation tactics and good conduct, setting them apart from some other police forces.[31]

While Italy's police force, particularly the Carabinieri, is generally respected, there are some issues. These include instances of corruption, abuse of power, and excessive use of force, particularly in protests or demonstrations. The treatment of migrants and refugees has also raised concerns, with reports of mistreatment and racial profiling. The militarized nature of the Carabinieri can sometimes lead to tensions, especially during public demonstrations. Additionally, issues like understaffing, limited resources, and concerns over accountability and transparency have been raised, which can affect the effectiveness and public trust in law enforcement.

If you wish to lodge a complaint against the Italian police, there are several avenues available to address grievances related to police conduct. You can report the issue to the police's internal affairs department (*Ufficio Affari Interni*), if it involves misconduct or abuse by officers. For criminal offenses, you can file a complaint with the local Public Prosecutor's Office (*Procura della Repubblica*). If the complaint concerns mistreatment in detention, you can contact the *National Ombudsman for the Rights of Detainees*. Human rights organizations like *Amnesty International* or *Associazione Antigone* can also provide assistance and advocacy. Additionally, you can report the issue directly to the local police station or the Carabinieri (112). For more serious or systemic issues, complaints can be made to the Ministry of the Interior, which oversees Italy's police forces. It is important to collect evidence and relevant details to support your complaint.

---

31 https://foreignpolicy.com/2020/06/10/
    american-cops-could-learn-a-lesson-from-italys-carabinieri/

 **General Questions**

1. *If I am convicted in Italy, am I likely to be released on bail pending the outcome of my appeal?* In Italy, there is no bail system. If convicted, release pending appeal is possible but not automatic. The judge will assess whether there is a risk of flight, tampering with evidence, or further criminal activity. If deemed a risk, you may be required to remain in detention. You can request release, but the judge's decision will depend on the circumstances, and you have the right to appeal if denied.

2. *Who is entitled to release pending appeal?* Those with strong ties, less serious crimes, or a potentially strong appeal are more likely to be granted release. However, individuals convicted of serious offenses or considered a flight risk may be denied release.

3. *If I am arrested, how soon will I see a judge or magistrate?* If you are arrested, you must see a judge within 48 hours.

4. *Will I be able to contact my country's embassy in Italy?* Yes. If you are arrested in Italy, you have the right to contact your country's embassy or consulate. Italian authorities are required to inform foreign nationals of their right to consular assistance, and the embassy can help with providing legal information, facilitating communication with family, and ensuring your well-being. While the embassy cannot provide legal representation or advice, it does maintain a list of English- speaking attorneys who are licensed to practice in different areas of law in Italy. This list can be accessed at https://it.usembassy.gov/u-s-citizen-services/attorneys/.

JAILS VS. PRISONS: CONDITIONS & CULTURE

JAILS VS. PRISONS: CONDITIONS & CULTURE

 **Overview**

The Italian prison system focuses on both punishment and rehabilitation, with an emphasis on reintegrating prisoners into society. It operates under a framework established by a 1975 law, which has been updated over time to address challenges like overcrowding and limited resources. The system is managed by the Ministry of Justice and is structured into regional branches, with prisons overseen by wardens, who are responsible for both security and rehabilitation. Prison police maintain internal security, while educators, social workers, and healthcare professionals provide rehabilitation and support.

Conditions in Italian prisons are often difficult, with overcrowding being a significant issue. Many prisons are housed in historical buildings, which can be outdated and poorly equipped. The strain on resources affects the quality of rehabilitation programs, which include education, vocational training, substance abuse treatment, and psychological support. Despite these challenges, Italy's prison system remains committed to the goal of rehabilitation, though the balance between punishment and reintegration can sometimes be difficult to achieve due to financial limitations and high inmate populations.

Jails vs. Prisons

In general, **jails** are used to hold people who are awaiting trial or sentencing, or who are serving short sentences. **Prisons** are used to house people who have been sentenced to long-term incarceration, reflecting the seriousness of their crimes.

Italian prisons have faced issues with overcrowding and inadequate facilities, which can lead to poor living conditions. Access to healthcare can also be limited, and there are concerns about the treatment and rights of inmates. However, some Italian prisons have implemented open-cell regimes that can help inmates with legal issues, and provide access to recreational and cultural areas, as well as assistance facilities.

Police Custody and Arrival at Prison[32]

There are three main police forces in Italy authorized to detain a person:

* the national police (*Polizia*)
* the national gendarmerie (*Carabinieri*)
* a militarized police force responsible for dealing with financial crimes and smuggling (*Guardia di Finanza*)

Arrest

Upon arrest, you have the right to be informed in your native language of the reason for your detention. If needed, an interpreter will be provided. Within 24 hours, the arresting officer must give you both a verbal and written notice of the charges against you. You also have the right to appoint a lawyer to represent you; until your lawyer arrives, you may choose not to speak. If you do not hire a lawyer, one will be appointed for you by the State, but you must cover the cost of their services. If you

---

32 https://www.gov.uk/government/publications/italy-prisoner-pack/ information-for-british-nationals-detained-or-imprisoned-in-italy

cannot afford a lawyer, you may be eligible for legal aid, although this may not cover initial services.

You will likely be held in police custody until a judge validates your arrest. During this time, you are entitled to humane treatment, including access to food, water, personal hygiene, and medical care if needed (at no cost).

You also have the right to a clean room with a bed, depending on how long you are detained. Additionally, you should be informed about the belongings taken from you and may notify a family member or other contact about your arrest (though phone calls may not be allowed). Finally, you can request to inform your consulate or embassy of your detention.

Appearing in Court

Within 96 hours of your arrest, you will appear before a judge for a hearing, during which the judge will determine whether your arrest was conducted lawfully. However, they will not provide any information about what will happen next. During the hearing, you may be questioned by the Public Prosecutor, the judge, or both. Your lawyer must be present, and while you are required to confirm your personal details—such as your name, date of birth, and place of birth—you are not obligated to answer all questions.

Arrival at Prison

Upon arrival at the prison, the Registration Office (*Ufficio Matricola*) will manage your intake, including maintaining your records and handling day-to-day regulations. This includes appointing a lawyer, forwarding legal documents, and managing visits.

You have the right to inform your family once the arrest paperwork is complete, or if you're transferred to another facility. You may choose one or two legal advisers, and while visits from your lawyer are allowed, you must submit a request to the Registration Office, which will schedule the visit. If the court has imposed restrictions on your contact with a lawyer at the time of arrest, you may be denied a visit for up to five days.

You will be fully searched, have your fingerprints taken, and you'll need to surrender any valuables, such as money and personal items. A written list of your deposited belongings will be provided.

You will also undergo a medical and psychological assessment, where you should inform staff of any health conditions or medications needed.

 **Prison Conditions and Daily Life**

Over-crowding can be a problem in prisons in Italy. The number of inmates to each cell depends on the size of the cell and the number of prisoners in a particular prison. There are usually three to six prisoners in a cell. Women's prisons are separate from men's.

If you experience harassment, threats, or violence while in prison, you should report this to the embassy or consulate as soon as possible. It is their responsibility to report any allegations of mistreatment against a foreign national. However, they will only raise concerns with the prison administration at your request.

Food

You will be provided with three meals a day (breakfast, lunch, and dinner). If you have special dietary needs due to health or religious reasons, inform the prison authorities. To supplement your diet, you will need funds to purchase extra food from the prison shop; here, a prisoner delegation will oversee meal preparation and the pricing of items.

You can request a list of available items from the Registration Office. Clean drinking water will be accessible, and personal gas cookers may be used in accordance with health and safety rules. You are also allowed to receive food parcels from outside, within specified weight limits.

Hygiene

Overcrowding in Italian prisons is a major contributor to several health issues, including the spread of infectious diseases and mental health problems. The overall hygiene conditions can also be poor. Showers are typically located in communal areas, and toiletries can be purchased from the prison shop.

You are allowed to receive personal items such as underwear, clothing, and bedding, but you are responsible for maintaining them. You must also keep your cell tidy and maintain personal cleanliness. All prisoners have access to regular showers and are provided with routine hair and beard cuts.

Work and Study

You can request to participate in work activities, both inside prison or outside. Whether you can work outside prison depends on the type of sentence being served and availability. The supervisory judge approves the work plan set out by the prison director and lists the obligations and rules that need to be followed. However, it is difficult for the prison to supply work to all prisoners because there are often not enough jobs to go around. This means you may have to wait a while before securing a suitable job. Note that the prison authorities are not obligated to offer you a job, and that sentenced prisoners will normally be prioritized over remanded prisoners. Prisoners will be financially compensated for their work and their wage credited to their prison account.

Primary and secondary Italian school courses are available in all prisons, however, not all prisons offer internal training courses, workshops, or rehabilitation programs. Some rewards are granted to prisoners who have shown commitment and merit in education and vocational training. You can take courses as a private student to get a high school diploma or a university degree. Prison facilities typically have a library, which is managed in partnership with some of the prisoners.

Exercise

Prisoners have access to cultural, sports and leisure activities. To participate in courses and other prison programs, you need to submit an application to the prison social worker or to the Registration Office.

During outdoor exercise time, prisoners are allowed to do some physical training and some prisons even have their own gym. Each prisoner has the right to spend at least two hours outdoors daily, or, under certain prison regimes, a shorter period of no less than one hour.

Religious Expression

Prisons in Italy acknowledge and uphold prisoners' right to practice their faith while in custody. Religious leaders may visit prisoners upon request.

Prisoner Demographics [33]

The most common crimes committed by inmates of both genders in Italy are drug crimes, robbery, and theft. Demographic data from 2022 on Italy's prison population shows that the largest group of prisoners are aged between 50 and 59 years, and most of them hold a lower secondary school diploma, typically a middle school certification.

On the other hand, inmates with a professional school degree or a university degree represent the smallest incarcerated population. Although women represent a relatively small fraction of all prisoners, there are a considerable number of mothers living in prisons with their children.

---

33 https://www.statista.com/topics/7628/prisons-in-italy/#topicOverview

Prisoner Self-Harm[34]

In addition to overcrowding, several other problems affect Italian penal institutions. Most notably, a considerable number of suicides among prisoners has highlighted concerns about the mental health of detainees.

The number of prisoner suicides in Italy peaked at 84 in 2022, with a steady increase in suicides and suicide attempts in recent years. The Italian prison system also faces criticism for the harsh conditions of Mafia prisoners. In 2019, the European Court of Human Rights (ECHR) ruled that the treatment of Mafia inmates violated their human rights and called for reforms.

As of July 2023, Italy's prison population exceeded the operational capacity of the prison system. Overcrowding is a significant issue, with some prisons operating at over 180% capacity. For example, a prison in Taranto, Southern Italy, was at 196.4% capacity, making it the most overcrowded facility in the country.

Rules and Regulations

All prisoners are required to adhere to the rules and regulations of prison life, as well as any specific instructions given by penitentiary staff. If you break the rules, you may face punishment, depending on the severity of the violation. Examples of infractions include failing to maintain cleanliness, not fulfilling work obligations, possessing or smuggling unauthorized items, money, or tools that could be used to harm yourself or others, making false communications either within the prison or with the outside world, engaging in bullying or violence, returning late from authorized leave, or committing any other offenses defined by law.

Punishments for violations can include a warning, a reprimand, exclusion from leisure and sports activities for up to ten days, isolation during outdoor exercise for up to ten days, or exclusion from all associated activities for up to fifteen days.

---

34   https://www.statista.com/topics/7628/prisons-in-italy/#topicOverview

Drugs are strictly prohibited in all Italian prisons, and severe penalties apply to those caught possessing, using, or trafficking drugs. Prisoners may also be subject to searches whenever deemed necessary for security reasons.

Smoking is permitted inside cells, in designated areas, and outdoors, but it is prohibited in communal indoor spaces.

Good behavior can lead to rewards, such as early release. For every six months served, prisoners who consistently follow the rules and participate in rehabilitation programs can have their sentence reduced by 45 days.

 ## General Questions[35]

1. *Can prisoners, who are foreign nationals, request contact and be granted reasonable means to communicate with the diplomatic or consular representatives of their country?* **Yes**, foreign prisoners can always request to have contact with the diplomatic or consular representatives of their country, and who visits them in prison. However, these representatives do not always come to visit.

2. *Are prisoners, who are foreign nationals, informed of the possibility of requesting that the execution of their sentence be transferred to another country?* **No.** Italian authorities do not automatically provide information about the possibility of serving a sentence in the country of origin (under the Strasbourg Convention) or about expulsion as an alternative to detention for individuals sentenced to less than two years. There is no explicit requirement for them to do so. However, educators or prison officers in the admissions office may occasionally offer this information.

---

35 https://www.prisonobservatory.org/upload/Italy_Peniten.pdf

3. *Are prisoners, who are foreign nationals, divided by country of origin within the sections of each institution?* **Yes,** whenever possible. The institution prefers to house prisoners who speak a common language together to prevent conflicts. However, the establishment of ethnic sections is generally avoided.

4. *Are interpreter services available to foreign nationals?* **Yes.** Although there are interpreters and cultural mediators available, their numbers are limited in relation to the many needs of prisoners. While the law does not mandate the use of cultural mediators, it recognizes the important role they play.

HELPING A FRIEND OR RELATIVE IMPRISONED IN ITALY

HELPING A FRIEND OR RELATIVE IMPRISONED IN ITALY

 **Friends and Family Visits**[36]

Before traveling to Italy, check with your home country's government for the latest travel advice, including information on safety and security, entry requirements, and any travel warnings.

If a friend or family member is awaiting trial in Italy, you must first obtain permission from the Preliminary Investigations Judge (*GIP-Giudice Indagini Preliminari*) in order for them to receive visits or make telephone calls to you or other relatives.

If a friend or family member has been sentenced, you must submit a visitation request to the prison director to be able to visit them. Your lawyer can give you further information and assist with the process.

Generally, only family members are allowed to visit, though exceptions may be made at the prison director's discretion. Common law partners may need to provide a legal declaration along with supporting evidence, such as phone bills or joint bank accounts.

---

36 https://www.gov.uk/government/publications/italy-prisoner-pack/information-for-british-nationals-detained-or-imprisoned-in-italy

Family members and third parties eligible for visits include:

- Spouses
- Cohabitant, regardless of sex
- Relatives within the fourth degree of kinship
- Individuals with valid reasons to meet the detainee

Prisoners are typically allowed up to six visits per month, but if convicted of a serious offense, they may be limited to four visits. Additional visits may be granted if the prisoner is seriously ill or if a child relative under 10 years of age requests to visit.

Each visit is usually limited to three people, though exceptions may apply for relatives or cohabitants. Visits typically last one hour, but if relatives travel from abroad, a request can be made for an extended visit of two to three hours, subject to approval by the prison director. Visiting days and times vary between prisons.

What to expect when you visit

Upon arrival, visitors will have their identification checked and will be required to deposit their personal belongings. They will also need to pass through a metal detector.

Spouses and family members, who are not EU citizens, must present a valid form of ID and a document issued by the Italian consulate in the country of origin, or document (translated into Italian) showing the family relationship.

Visits typically take place in designated areas, where they are visually monitored by the prison officers. Most prisons in Italy also have vending machines offering snacks and drinks for visitors.

What can you bring on your visit?

You can bring packages containing food, clothing, and various other approved items. The total weight should not exceed a monthly allowance of 20 kilos (26.46 lbs).

Form 176, available at the prison Registry, lists the items that friends or family members can send to a prisoner. This list may vary between prisons, so it's advisable to check with the Registration Office or the embassy/consulate for specific details.

Certain items are considered dangerous and are not allowed to be sent to prisoners, including liquids (such as toiletries), beverages, tobacco, and food in glass, metal, or aluminum packaging. Military-style clothing and hooded garments are also prohibited. Some items, such as medication and belts (without buckles), require prior authorization.

All packages are inspected before being delivered to prisoners, and any banned items will be confiscated.

 **Receiving Money**

There are several ways a prisoner may be able to receive financial assistance while in prison:

- **Private funds:** deposited by family and friends.

- **"Prisoners Abroad" stipend:** depending on where you are detained, if your family cannot support you financially, "Prisoners Abroad" may be able to send you a small grant every quarter for essentials (enough for one hot meal a day).

- **Postal Order:** If your relatives live in Italy, they can send a postal order (*bollettino postale*) addressed to the prison administration, including the prisoner's full name and the purpose of the payment (*causal*). The prison administration will then deposit the amount into the prisoner's personal account. Each prison has a Current Accounts Office for this purpose.

- **Over the counter delivery during visits:** amounts permitted vary from prison to prison according to internal regulations.

- **Bank Transfer:** A bank transfer can also be made to the prison's account, using the provided IBAN and SWIFT codes. The reason for the payment (causal) should include the prisoner's full name. This option, however, is not available in all prisons.

Letters and Parcels

Prisoners have a right to unlimited letter correspondence while serving their sentence. Depending on the sentence, incoming and outgoing mail may be censored. Mail is subject to examination and delays are to be expected.

Friends and family should send mail and parcels directly to the prison. Embassies/consulates are not able to forward mail on your behalf. All parcels are opened and checked by prison staff before they are handed over to prisoners. A prisoner can receive four postal parcels per month. There is a weight limit of five kilos (11.02 lbs) per parcel, but this depends on whether a person has received other packages that month, or during ordinary prison visits. Educational material, such as books and magazines, do not count toward the weight limit.

Prison regulations state there must be a 15-day delay between parcels delivered during visits and parcels received by post. Excessive parcels are either returned to the sender, at the prisoner's expense, or kept in the prison's storeroom. A copy of goods permitted in a particular prison can be requested from the prison directly.

The sender of a letter or parcel must ensure that the prisoner's full name (as known to the prison) is written on the envelope, along with the name and address of the prison and return information.

Parcels sent to Italy from outside the EU may incur customs charges. If a parcel arrives with such charges, the prisoner will be given the opportunity to pay them, provided they have enough funds in their prison account. Customs checks may also result in significant delays in the delivery of parcels.

Telephone Calls

The prisoner does not have an automatic right to make a phone call. To make a call, domestic or international, they must first obtain permission from the judge.

Once in prison, they can make calls to relatives and partners, and in some cases, to friends and acquaintances. To request a call, they must submit a written request to the prison director, providing proof of their relationship with the person they wish to contact, such as a marriage certificate, a copy of the telephone bill for the number they want to call, and a copy of the bill owner's passport.

Prisoners are allowed one call per week, with each call lasting no longer than ten minutes, and calls must be made within designated time slots. Calls are made through the prison's switchboard operator. **Mobile phones are not permitted in prison.**

Family and friends are responsible for the cost of phone calls, and they can purchase phone cards to cover these charges. To request visits or phone calls, they must apply to the court if the prisoner is awaiting trial, or to the prison director if the prisoner has been sentenced.

Prisoners cannot receive incoming calls.

Mobile Phones

A prisoner may only call a mobile phone under specific conditions:

- If they have not had any type of visit or contact for at least 15 days

- If they have no other means of contact

Skype and Video Calls

Some prisons allow the use of Skype for video calls. For more information, check with your country's embassy or consulate to find out if the prison where your friend or family member is being held offers this option. In some prisons, video calls may also be allowed via Teams or WhatsApp to help maintain family relationships.

General Questions[37]

1. *How do I find out where my family member/friend is being held?* You can contact your country's embassy or consulate in Italy. Your friend or family member may have asked the police or the prison staff to inform them already. Some countries have special agreements with Italy, ensuring that their embassy or consulate is automatically notified in the event of an arrest.

2. *How can I communicate with the prisoner?* Prisoners have the right to unlimited correspondence, though mail may be censored based on the charges. Mobile phones are prohibited; inmates use telephone cards instead. To make a call, prisoners must get permission from the judge and the Prison Governor, submitting a written request with a phone bill, the bill holder's passport, and proof of their relationship to the person they wish to contact. International calls require verification by consular authorities.

---

37 https://www.prison-insider.com/en/italie/
en-cas-d-arrestation-57632aa031c75

3. ***What steps do I need to take to visit my loved one in prison?***
Pre-trial detainees must apply to the investigating judge for visitation, while sentenced detainees must apply to the Registration Office. Prisoners are allowed up to six one-hour visits per month, with a maximum of three visitors at a time.

All visitors must be authorized, with third-party visits subject to prison management's approval. Visitors must provide ID and undergo security checks. Individuals with pending criminal charges cannot visit. **Note that conjugal visits are not allowed in Italy.**

4. ***Am I allowed to send a parcel? If so, what can it contain?*** **Yes,** you can send parcels to someone in prison, with a limit of four per month, each weighing up to five kilos (or 11.02 lbs), totaling 20 kilos (or 44.09 lbs). Books, newspapers, and literature are usually exempt from weight limits. Prohibited items include alcohol, drugs, and anything dangerous. All parcels are inspected, and there's a 15-day delay between those delivered during visits and those sent by mail. Check with the prison for a list of approved items before sending.

THE ADMINISTRATION OF JUSTICE

THE ADMINISTRATION OF JUSTICE

Overview

The administration of justice is how the judicial system handles criminal and civil cases. It's also known as criminal procedure for criminal cases and civil procedure for non-criminal cases. This process follows formal rules, including the right to bail in criminal cases, how evidence is presented, and how guilt or innocence is determined by a judge or jury.

Italy's judicial system is based on civil law. Judges and public prosecutors carry out judicial duties, while the Ministry of Justice manages administrative tasks. The judicial system is divided into areas such as civil, criminal, administrative, accounting, military, and taxation law. Magistrates, which include judges and prosecutors, have jurisdiction over civil and criminal cases. Judges oversee trials, while prosecutors investigate cases.

 **Administration of Courts**[38]

The Italian Constitution designates the Ministry of Justice to oversee court administration because of its close relationship with the judiciary. Magistrates are assigned to courts based on their preferences after passing a tough public exam. They cannot be reassigned, promoted, removed, or disciplined without approval from the *Consiglio Superiore della Magistratura* (CSM), which ensures their independence. The CSM, chaired by the President of the Republic, oversees all matters related to magistrates.

The Ministry of Justice operates at two levels: centrally in Rome with local branches for specific areas, and within judicial offices, tribunals, and courts. It also manages judicial service personnel.

At the highest courts or public prosecution offices, a chief magistrate oversees the judiciary and makes final decisions. A court manager (*dirigente*) organizes judicial services and supports judges and prosecutors, holding the highest position among administrative staff.

 Types of Courts

In Italy, the judicial system is structured around different types of courts, each with specific areas of competence. The main types of courts are:

1. Ordinary Courts:

- **Court of First Instance** (**Tribunale**): Handles both civil and criminal cases. It is the main court for most legal matters, including family disputes, property cases, and criminal trials.

---

38 https://e-justice.europa.eu/content_judicial_systems_in_member_states-16-it-en.do?member=1

- **Court of Appeals** (**Corte d'Appello**): Handles appeals against decisions made by lower courts (Tribunali). It reviews both civil and criminal cases and can either confirm, modify, or overturn the original ruling.

- **Supreme Court of Cassation** (**Corte di Cassazione**): The highest court in Italy, which primarily hears appeals on points of law. It does not review the facts of a case, only whether the law has been applied correctly. Its decisions are final.

2. Administrative Courts:

- **Regional Administrative Courts** (**Tribunali Amministrativi Regionali, TAR**): Handle disputes involving public administration, including challenges to administrative acts or decisions made by governmental bodies.

- **Council of State** (**Consiglio di Stato**): The highest court for administrative matters. It hears appeals from TARs and has an advisory role to the government on administrative legal matters.

3. Accounting Courts:

- **Court of Auditors** (**Corte dei Conti**): Oversees the legality of public spending and state finances. It has jurisdiction over cases of financial mismanagement or misconduct in public administration.

4. Military Courts:

- **Military Court** (**Corte Marziale**): Handles cases involving military personnel and offenses related to military discipline or crimes committed within the military context.

5. Tax Courts:

- **Tax Commissions** (**Commissioni Tributarie**): Deal with disputes related to taxation, such as disagreements between taxpayers and the tax authorities.

Each of these courts plays a specific role in the Italian judicial system, ensuring that legal issues are handled by the appropriate specialized body.

 **Law of the Land True Story**

The case of Amanda Knox, an American student accused and later acquitted of murdering her roommate in Italy, drew global attention not only for its sensational details but also for the broader issues of crime and the legal system in Italy. Knox's conviction and subsequent release highlighted concerns about the Italian justice system, including the length of trials, the use of circumstantial evidence, and the influence of media coverage on legal proceedings. While Knox's case remains controversial, it also serves as a reminder of the complexities of criminal investigations in Italy, where cases can sometimes be marked by high public scrutiny, slow legal processes, and the challenges of ensuring fair trials. Her case, along with others, has contributed to ongoing discussions about the balance between swift justice and the protection of individual rights, shaping how both locals and foreigners perceive crime and the legal system in Italy.

CRIME VICTIM ASSISTANCE

CRIME VICTIM ASSISTANCE

Worldwide Victim Assistance

While the United Nations has set out fundamental rights for crime victims, the responsibility for implementing these rights lies with individual countries. As a result, the support and services available to victims of crime vary significantly from one country to another, influenced by factors such as culture, social norms, and economic conditions. This means that the level of assistance and the approach to victim support can be quite different, depending on where the crime occurs.

As a foreign national in Italy, you have the same rights as any domestic victim of a crime. These rights include free interpretation services during police questioning, court proceedings, and when receiving important information about your case. You are also entitled to have documents translated, such as the confirmation of your report or complaint. Additionally, you have the right to be present at court hearings, make statements, and submit evidence. You can participate in the judicial process either personally or through a legal representative. If applicable, you may be entitled to compensation from the offender or state funds to cover medical expenses, legal fees, and other damages resulting from the crime.

If you are a U.S. citizen who is a victim of crime abroad, you may experience physical, emotional, or financial harm. Resources and assistance vary by country and crime type, so it's important to check the country information page for your destination. You can contact the nearest U.S. embassy or consulate, or the U.S. Department of State's Office of Overseas Citizens Services for support. For emergency help, call (**888**) **407-4747** (U.S. or Canada) or (**202**) **501-4444** (from overseas). Consular officers are available 24/7.[39]

Reporting a Crime[40]

If you are a victim of crime in Italy, it is important to file a criminal complaint immediately. You can do this at the main police station (Questura), any nearby Carabinieri or Polizia station, or online via the "denuncia via web" service at **https://www.poliziadistato.it/articolo/1095**.

While filing a report is not always mandatory, it is required in certain situations. The report should include details about the crime, the offender (if known), and any evidence. If you do not know the perpetrator, you can file a report against "persons unknown," and the police will conduct an investigation.

A **complaint** is necessary if you want the offender to be prosecuted for a non-publicly actionable offense. It must describe the crime and express your desire for legal action. Complaints can be withdrawn, except in cases of sexual assault or offenses involving minors, but withdrawal requires the accused's acceptance.

If you are involved in a private dispute, you can file a **petition**. Police will attempt to mediate, and if a crime is discovered, they will report it to the judicial authorities. Complaints, reports, and petitions can be submitted at police stations, provincial police offices, or directly to the public prosecutor.

---

39 https://travel.state.gov/content/travel/en/international-travel/emergencies/crime.html#:~:text=Contact%20the%20nearest%20U.S.%20embassy,day%2C%207%20days/week

40 https://faq.unisr.it/en/i-have-been-the-victim-of-a-crime.-what-should-i-do

After filing a report, you will receive information about your rights and role in the legal process. You will be informed on how to track updates on your case, your involvement in the investigation and trial, and your right to be notified about the trial date, location, and charges. If you join the proceedings as a civil party, you will also receive the judgment summary. You will be updated on the case status, entries in the Official Registry of Reported Offenses, and any request to close the case. If your rights are violated, you will be informed about how to challenge it. You may also settle the case by withdrawing the complaint or through mediation, if applicable.

If you experience theft or lose a valuable item while in Italy, you must file a **theft/loss report** (*denuncia di furto/smarrimento*) with the local authorities. Reporting the theft is important for official documentation, especially if you intend to seek compensation from a hotel, insurance company, or other parties. If authorities recover your stolen or lost item, they will contact you.

Legal Aid

After contacting the prosecuting authorities, you will be informed in a language you understand about your right to legal advice and state-funded legal aid, if you meet certain financial criteria. Legal aid is available to individuals whose income is below €11,369.24 (US$11,917.24), with additional allowances for dependents. This applies to both Italian citizens and foreign nationals. If eligible, you can apply for legal aid shortly after filing a report with the authorities.

Once the investigation begins, you will be notified of your right to a defense lawyer. If you cannot afford one, the court will appoint a defense attorney at no cost. You also have the right to choose your own lawyer, but if you do not qualify for legal aid, you will be required to pay for court-appointed counsel. Additionally, you are entitled to an interpreter and document translation if necessary.

Free legal aid is guaranteed under Italy's Constitution (Article 24) and covers all stages of criminal and related civil cases. Victims of certain sexual offenses, such as sexual violence, are exempt from income limits, and individuals facing arrest or detention can also access free legal aid, regardless of income. To qualify, your income must be below the specified limit, but allowances are made for each dependent you have. Legal aid is available to both Italian citizens and foreigners, including minors and stateless individuals.

Victims' Rights and Obligations

As a witness, you are required to attend the hearing and follow the judge's instructions, answering questions truthfully. However, you are not obligated to disclose anything that could lead to self-incrimination. If you are unable to attend the hearing, you must inform the court in advance with a valid reason. If your absence is justified, the judge may reschedule your appearance. Failure to appear without a valid reason may result in compulsory attendance, fines, and the costs incurred by your absence.

You are obligated to answer questions truthfully, and refusing to answer, providing false statements, or withholding information can lead to penalties under Article 372 of the Italian Penal Code, including a prison sentence. However, a witness cannot be detained during a hearing. If you correct a false statement or confirm the truth before the judgment, you will not face criminal charges. No punishment applies if you give false testimony to protect yourself or a close relative from criminal conviction.

Victims' Compensation[41]

In Italy, compensation can be claimed for intentional offenses involving violence, unlawful labor exploitation, and certain severe personal injuries. This includes medical and assistance costs, with fixed compensation amounts for specific crimes, such as sexual assault, homicide, or disfigurement. Compensation covers medical treatment, additional

---

41 https://e-justice.europa.eu/491/EN/
if_my_claim_is_to_be_considered_in_this_country?ITALY&member=1

care, permanent injury, loss of earnings, and expenses related to legal proceedings.

Claims must be filed within 60 days after the offense is recognized or a criminal conviction becomes final. Compensation amounts are set by law, with specific amounts for certain crimes:

- **Homicide:** €50,000 (US$52,410)
- **Sexual assault:** €25,000 (US$26,205)
- **Serious personal injury or facial disfigurement:** €25,000 (US$26,205).

Compensation can also cover stolen or damaged property, psychological damage, and pain and suffering.

 ## General Questions

1. *Am I entitled to free interpreting services during investigation and trial?* **Yes.** You are entitled to free interpreting services during both the investigation and trial stages, if you do not speak or understand Italian. This ensures that you can fully understand the proceedings and communicate effectively with law enforcement, legal authorities, and the court. The right to interpretation also extends to translated documents, ensuring that all necessary legal information is accessible to you in your language.

2. *Who provides victim support?* Support is provided to victims of crime by the healthcare facilities in the region, by residential facilities, refuges, shelters, and other facilities managed by local and regional organizations. Many regions have a network of associations consisting of local organizations, the public prosecutor's offices, district courts, and health services, which offer free support to victims of any kind of offense.

3. *Will the police automatically refer me to the victim support services?* **Yes**, especially if you are a victim of specific offenses, such as sex trafficking, domestic abuse, or sexual assault. There are established organizations working closely with law enforcement that can provide you with information about shelters or residential facilities to support your care and safety.

Law Of The Land True Story

On January 24, 2019, the European Court of Human Rights (ECHR) issued a ruling requiring Italy to compensate Amanda Knox with €18,400 (approximately US$20,800) for a violation of her rights during the critical hours following her arrest in Perugia in 2007. The court determined that Italian authorities had failed to ensure Knox had access to a lawyer or a competent interpreter when she was initially detained. This failure occurred during a period when she was questioned without proper legal representation, and she was not adequately informed of her rights due to the language barrier.

The ECHR found that these actions violated Knox's right to a fair trial and her rights under the European Convention on Human Rights, particularly regarding access to legal assistance and the need for competent interpretation during police interrogations.

Knox, an American citizen, had been arrested in connection with the murder of her British roommate, Meredith Kercher, and was later acquitted of all charges. The ruling served as a reminder of the fundamental protections offered to individuals under the European human rights framework, including the right to a fair trial and the right to communicate effectively with legal authorities.

POLICE

- Law Enforcement in Italy
- General Questions
- Law of the Land Hypothetical

POLICE

Law Enforcement in Italy[42]

Law and order in Italy is the responsibility of five national police forces and two local police forces. Together, these organizations employ over 300,000 officers, the highest number employed by any of the EU countries.

The two local forces include the **Provincial Police** (*Polizia Provinciale*), which is responsible for enforcing national and local hunting and fishing laws as well as some traffic regulations, and the **Municipal Police** (*Polizia Municipale*), which is responsible for enforcing local regulations, traffic control, and investigating petty crimes. In some regions, the Provincial Police and the Municipal Police are referred to as the "Local Police" (Polizia Locale).

The five national forces are:

- **State Police** (**Polizia di Stato**): a civilian force focused on public order and security, operating under the Department of Public Security. It has about 110,000 personnel and includes specialized divisions like highway patrol, railway security, postal and internet crimes, and border controls.

---

42 https://www.understandingitaly.com/italian-police.html

- **Finance Police (Guardia di Finanza:** an Italian military force with around 70,000 officers, operating under the Ministry of Economy and Finance. It handles financial crimes like bribery, money laundering, fraud, cybercrime, and counterfeiting. Additionally, it collaborates with the State Police and Carabinieri on border control issues, investigating illegal immigration, smuggling, and international drug trafficking.

- **Military Police (Arma dei Carabinieri:** Italy's national military police force, controlled by the Ministry of Defense, with both military and civil duties. About 80% of the Carabinieri are stationed across Italy in regional and provincial commands. They also run the Specialist Mobile Unit for public order and emergencies, and the elite ROS unit, which handles complex crimes like the Mafia, terrorism, and subversive activities, with a presence in every city.

- **Prison Police (Polizia Penitenziaria):** manages Italy's prison system, under the Ministry of Justice. Their duties include maintaining order, protecting prisoners, preventing escapes, transporting inmates to court and to medical facilities, and overseeing work and education programs.

- **Forestry Police (Corpo Forestale dello Stato):** protects Italy's natural resources, under the Ministry of Agriculture direction, including national parks, forests, and endangered species. It enforces environmental laws and combats crimes like poaching and illegal food production. It also assists in mountain operations and disaster relief.

In addition, *Direzione Investigativa Antimafia* (DIA), or the Anti-Mafia Investigation Department, is a cooperative venture between all five of the police forces charged with tackling organized crime.

In case of an emergency in Italy, dial 112, which is the universal emergency number. It's a free call, and the operator will connect you to the appropriate service or authority. A list of emergency/important numbers can be found at the end of this book.

 **General Questions**

1. *Are random police stops legal in Italy?* **Yes**, random police stops are legal in Italy. If stopped by the police, you are required to provide your personal information, such as your name, surname, date and place of birth, nationality, and residency— basically, the details found on your ID card. However, you are not obligated to hand over your ID card, if you choose not to. Refusing to provide your personal information or providing false information is considered a crime.

2. *How long can I be held by the police?* The maximum duration is up to 96 hours. Specifically, within 24 hours of an arrest or detention, the police must present the individual to the Public Prosecutor and submit all relevant documents (such as the arrest report and notes). The Public Prosecutor must then request validation of the detention within 48 hours. Following this, the judge must schedule a hearing to confirm the detention and make a decision within 48 hours of receiving the Prosecutor's request.

3. *Am I obligated to answer questions if arrested?* **No**. The individual, who is arrested or in custody, has the right to remain silent without facing any negative consequences for exercising this right. This right must be explicitly explained to them by the judicial authority before the interrogation begins.

 **Law of the Land Hypothetical**

HYPOTHETICAL: *Al Dente was staying at an Airbnb in Florence while visiting Italy when he heard the doorbell ring. When Mr. Dente answered the door, he was greeted by three women displaying police badges. They requested his passport and asked him to fill out a questionnaire. Is this a typical procedure in Italy?*

ANSWER: **No.** *However, in Italy, it is required by law for hotels and Airbnbs to report the personal details of each guest to the police. They must submit basic information from your ID (such as ID number, name, nationality, date of birth, check-in/check-out dates, etc.) through an online portal.*

CHAPTER 16

HOW TO GET LEGAL HELP IN ITALY

HOW TO GET LEGAL HELP IN ITALY

Overview

As a visitor in Italy, if you need legal help, there are several options available. You can seek assistance from local lawyers, many of whom offer services in English or other languages, especially in major cities. If you cannot afford legal fees, you may qualify for legal aid, provided you meet certain financial criteria. Additionally, consulates or embassies can offer guidance or refer you to trusted legal professionals. It's important to address legal issues promptly, as the Italian legal system may differ significantly from that of your home country.

Finding a Qualified Attorney

To find a qualified attorney as a visitor in Italy, you can start by contacting your embassy or consulate, which may provide a list of trusted, English-speaking lawyers. You can also use online directories like the *Ordine degli Avvocati* or legal platforms such as **Avvocatodelcittadino. it** to search for lawyers by location and specialty.

Asking for recommendations from local hotels, tourism offices, or expat groups can also be helpful. Additionally, some legal aid organizations offer referrals to lawyers who assist foreigners. Ensure that the lawyer is registered with the local bar association (*Ordine degli Avvocati*) and licensed to practice in Italy. It's a good idea to consult multiple lawyers to find one who best suits your needs.

 The United States Embassy maintains a list that contains the names and phone numbers of local English-speaking attorneys in Italy. You can find this list at **https://it.usembassy.gov/u-s-citizen-services/attorneys/**

Applying for Legal Aid

Legal aid in Italy is available to Italian citizens, non-Italian citizens, and stateless individuals who meet certain eligibility criteria. In criminal cases, non-citizens can apply for legal aid regardless of their residency status. However, **for civil and administrative cases, applicants must be residents of Italy.**

To apply for legal aid in criminal cases, you can contact the court where the case is being heard. For civil or administrative cases, applications should be made through the local bar association in the area where the relevant court is located.

Additionally, you can contact the *Crisis Unit*'s phone line at 06-491115 for further information, with services available daily.

Legal Aid in Italy[43]

In Italy, legal aid is available to non-citizens in criminal cases, regardless of their residency, while residency is required for civil and administrative cases. Applications for legal aid in criminal cases are made to the court

---

43 https://canestrinilex.com/en/readings/legal-aid-in-italy/#:~:text=In%20criminal%20cases%20legal%20aid,in%20the%20country%20is%20required.&text=The%20fees%20paid%20to%20the,court%20that%20decided%20the%20case

handling the case, while in other cases, they are addressed to the local bar association.

Once granted legal aid, the beneficiary can choose their attorney, provided the lawyer is registered for legal aid with the Court of Appeals in the relevant district. Attorneys must meet certain requirements, such as being a bar member for at least two years. Fees for legal aid attorneys are set by the court, typically capped at a percentage of the standard fees, with a 33% reduction by law (and often higher reductions in practice).

To qualify for legal aid in Italy, you must demonstrate that your taxable income is below €12,838 (US$13,470.91) for 2024. This threshold increases by €1,032.91 (US$1,083.83) for each additional family member living with you.

Required Documentation[44]

To apply for legal aid in Italy, non-EU citizens must provide several documents, including a **copy of their tax code** (*Codice fiscale*), **permit of stay** (*Permesso di soggiorno*), and **family status** (*Stato di famiglia*), if applicable. They may also need to **self-certify their income**, provide **certification from their consular authority**, and submit a **request for legal aid**.

Additional personal details, such as name, birth date, and residence, as well as household income from the previous year, must be included. Applicants must also commit to reporting any changes in income after submitting the application. Other supporting documents may be required, such as information about the next hearing and the opposing party's details. Applications can be made in person, by registered mail, or through a defender who authenticates the signature. After submission, a legal aid advocate will evaluate the case through a merits test and a means test to determine eligibility for legal aid.

---

44 https://tinyurl.com/4k8sp2w3

General Questions

1. *What do you write in the application for legal aid?* In the
   application for legal aid, non-EU citizens must declare both their
   Italian and foreign income. The application must be signed by
   the applicant, with the signature certified by a lawyer or the official receiving the application. For cases before other courts, the
   applicant must provide a clear statement of the facts and reasons
   for the case, along with any relevant evidence to support the
   grounds for the action.

2. *Which documents must be attached?* Italian and EU citizens
   don't need additional certifications for income declarations.
   Non-EU citizens must provide consular certification to verify
   their income claim, unless self-certification is accepted due to
   lack of documentation.

   Non-EU citizens under arrest or sentenced can submit the
   consular certification within 20 days, either directly or through
   a lawyer or relative. After submission, the judge or bar association may request proof of the income declaration or additional
   self-certification, if documentation is unavailable.

3. *How do you choose a Legal Aid lawyer?* Only one lawyer can be
   appointed for legal aid, and the chosen lawyer must be a member
   of the bar association in the region where the trial is being held.
   The lawyer must also be listed on the special list of legal aid lawyers, which can be accessed through the local bar association.

 **Law of the Land Hypothetical**

HYPOTHETICAL: *Maria is a non-EU citizen living in Italy on a temporary visa. She is facing criminal charges related to a minor traffic violation and needs legal assistance. Maria's income is below the required threshold for legal aid, and she doesn't have sufficient documentation to prove her income from her home country. Can she apply for legal aid, and what steps must she follow?*

ANSWER: **Yes**, *Maria can apply for legal aid in Italy, as non-EU citizens are eligible for legal aid in criminal cases, regardless of residency. She must declare both her Italian and foreign income, and if she can't provide documentation for her foreign income, she can self-certify it. Maria needs to complete the application, sign it, and have her signature certified by a lawyer or official. After submission, the court may request additional evidence or self-certification. If approved, Maria can choose a lawyer from the local bar association's legal aid list to represent her.*

CHAPTER 17
MEDICAL FACILITIES & HOSPITALS

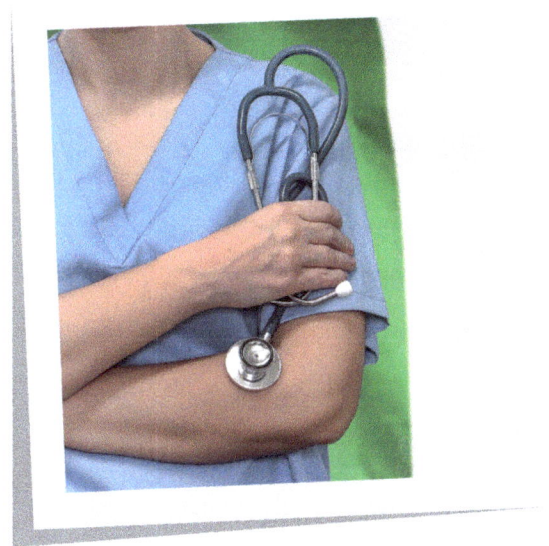

IN THIS CHAPTER

- Overview
- Visitors' Access to Healthcare in Italy
- Getting a Doctor's Appointment
- Medical Facilities for Foreign Visitors
- General Questions

MEDICAL FACILITIES & HOSPITALS

Overview[45]

When traveling to Italy, it's important to familiarize yourself with the healthcare system and know the locations of medical facilities in case of illness or injury.

In Italy, you can choose between public and private hospitals. Public hospitals offer both emergency and non-emergency services, with emergency care typically being free or requiring a small fee, depending on the hospital's policy. Non-emergency services at public hospitals are generally charged.

While public hospitals in Italy may have different quality standards compared to American hospitals, they must meet specific legal requirements and are typically well-equipped to handle emergencies.

 In case of an emergency, you can reach immediate medical assistance or request an ambulance by dialing 112, or 118, which works throughout Italy and Europe without needing a country code.

---

45 https://it.usembassy.gov/u-s-citizen-services/doctors/

Private hospitals in Italy typically do not have emergency rooms. Admission usually requires prior arrangements with the hospital administration or an affiliated doctor. Fees at private hospitals are generally higher than at public hospitals, and patients are expected to pay upfront before leaving, though those with insurance may seek reimbursement. Some private hospitals are "accredited," meaning that patients who are official residents of Italy and registered with the National Health Service may have their fees reimbursed.

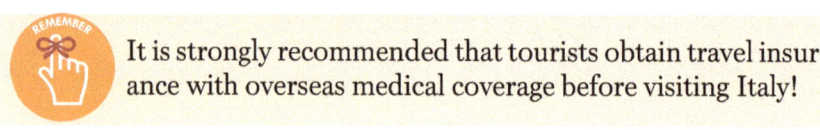

It is strongly recommended that tourists obtain travel insurance with overseas medical coverage before visiting Italy!

Visitors' Access to Healthcare in Italy[46]

Access to healthcare in Italy for foreigners varies based on nationality and the purpose of the visit:

- **EU Citizens:** EU citizens can access essential healthcare services in Italy through the European Health Insurance Card (EHIC), which covers necessary medical treatments during their stay. It's important to carry the EHIC card at all times.

- **Non-EU Citizens:** Non-EU visitors may not have the same healthcare rights, though emergency services are generally available to all. It is highly recommended that non-EU travelers have comprehensive travel insurance covering medical expenses, including non-urgent care. Emergency room visits in Italy tend to be relatively affordable.

- **Long-Term Residents:** Foreigners living in Italy long-term may be eligible to register with the National Health Service (SSN). This typically requires payment of a fee and meeting certain residency criteria, such as having stable employment or being enrolled in school.

---

46 https://www.pyllola.com/post/
healthcare-for-foreigners-and-tourists-in-italy

If you need medical intervention while visiting Italy, you have several options for medical care:

1. For emergencies, dial 112 or go directly to the nearest hospital emergency room (*Pronto Soccorso*).

2. For non-emergencies, you can visit a local pharmacy, use telemedicine services to consult a general practitioner or go to a walk-in clinic.

Emergency services are available to everyone, but non-EU tourists may be billed for these services afterward. Emergency room visits typically cost between €50 (US$52.46) and €200 (US$209.86) for basic care, with costs rising for more complex treatments or hospital admissions.

Free medical care is generally not available to tourists in Italy, and non-EU visitors are expected to cover their medical expenses. Be sure to keep all receipts, as you may be able to claim reimbursement through your travel insurance.

Getting a Doctor's Appointment

For tourists in Italy, the easiest ways to book a doctor's appointment are:

- **Online Booking Services:** Use platforms that allow you to book appointments with English-speaking doctors.

- **Hotel Recommendations:** Ask your hotel staff for advice on nearby doctors or clinics.

- **Walk-in Clinics:** Visit a local walk-in clinic for immediate care without an appointment.

- **Telemedicine:** Telemedicine has become a popular and practical solution for tourists seeking medical advice in Italy. Services like Pyllola Health offer access to English-speaking doctors, including general practitioners and specialists, without the need for registration or software downloads. This service, which became more widely used during the COVID-19 pandemic, allows travelers to receive medical advice for non-emergency issues almost instantly via video consultation. Doctors can also prescribe medications, which can be filled at any pharmacy in Italy. Additionally, telemedicine services typically offer prescriptions at lower fees, which is helpful if you've lost or forgotten your medications.

Medical Facilities for Foreign Visitors

Italy has several renowned medical facilities that are known for their high standards of care, particularly in major cities. For visitors, these hospitals are often the best choices due to their advanced technology, English-speaking staff, and experience in handling international patients:

- **Ospedale San Raffaele (Milan):** One of Italy's leading private hospitals, it is internationally recognized for its cutting-edge medical research, specialized treatments, and high-quality care. It is a popular choice for foreign patients, especially in fields like oncology, cardiology, and neurology.

- **Policlinico Universitario A. Gemelli (Rome):** This is one of Italy's largest and most prestigious teaching hospitals, affiliated with the Catholic University of the Sacred Heart. It offers a wide range of services, including emergency care, specialized surgeries, and complex treatments, and is known for its international patient care.

- **Istituto Clinico Humanitas (Milan) :** A well-known hospital offering both emergency services and specialized care in fields such as orthopedics, oncology, cardiology, and neurology. It has English-speaking staff and is recognized for its modern facilities and high-quality patient care.

- **Ospedale Niguarda (Milan):** A top public hospital in Milan, known for providing high-quality emergency care, trauma surgery, and advanced diagnostic services. It has a reputation for treating both locals and foreign patients.

- **Ospedale Città di Bologna (Bologna):** This is a large, well-equipped public hospital offering a broad range of medical services, including emergency care, surgery, and specialized treatments. Bologna's central location also makes it accessible for travelers in the northern part of the country.

- **Policlinico di Milano (Milan):** A major public teaching hospital in Milan with a wide range of services, including advanced surgery, cardiology, and reproductive medicine. The hospital offers excellent care and is particularly experienced in handling foreign patients.

- **Careggi University Hospital (Florence):** A well-regarded academic hospital in Tuscany that offers a broad spectrum of medical services, including emergency care, specialized treatments, and surgery. It is equipped with modern facilities and serves both locals and international patients.

- **Ospedale Sant'Andrea (Rome):** A major teaching hospital with expertise in cardiology, neurology, and trauma care. It is known for its patient-focused care and has English-speaking staff to assist international patients.

For visitors, it's important to have travel insurance to cover medical expenses and to verify if the hospital accepts international insurance or offers direct billing to insurance providers.

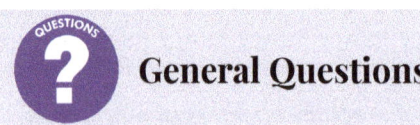 **General Questions**

1. ***Do foreigners need health insurance in Italy?*** While not legally required, health insurance is strongly recommended for foreigners visiting Italy. It can cover unexpected medical expenses and potential evacuation costs.

2. ***Do I need to have travel insurance?*** [47] While travel insurance is not a mandatory requirement for entering Italy or other Schengen countries for stays of less than 90 days, it is strongly recommended, especially for tourists. Travel insurance provides valuable protection against unexpected costs, such as medical emergencies, trip cancellations, lost luggage, and travel delays.

   For travelers engaging in adventure sports or outdoor activities, such as hiking, skiing, or boating, insurance can offer additional peace of mind by covering potential accidents or injuries. Additionally, if you're a non-EU citizen, having travel insurance that includes medical coverage is advisable, as healthcare in Italy can be expensive without insurance, and you may need it for emergencies.

---

47   https://www.marketwatch.com/guides/travel-insurance/italy/

DRIVING IN ITALY

DRIVING IN ITALY

Overview[48]

To drive in Italy, you must be at least 18 years old and hold a valid driving license. The required documents vary depending on whether you're driving a vehicle from an EU or non-EU country.

For cars registered in an EU country, the mandatory documents are:

- Vehicle registration certificate
- Valid driving license
- Insurance policy

For cars registered in a non-EU country, you must carry:

- Vehicle registration certificate
- Driving license issued by a non-EU country
- International driving license or a sworn translation of your license

---

48 https://www.italia.it/en/italy/things-to-do/tutto-quello-che-ce-da-sa-pere-per-guidare-in-italia-regole-stradali-consigli-e-informazi-oni-utili#:~:text=To%20drive%20in%20Italy%20you,Registration%20certificate

- Green card or temporary border insurance policy (check with your insurer)
- A sticker displaying the country code of your origin

The same documentation requirements apply for motorbikes.

Additionally, it is mandatory to wear a helmet that is approved by the EU when riding a motorbike in Italy.

Renting a Vehicle in Italy

Renting a car in Italy is a convenient way to explore the country, especially in areas where public transportation is limited. To rent a car, you must be at least 18 years old, though many companies set the minimum age at 21 or 25. A valid driver's license is required, and non-EU citizens may need an International Driving Permit (IDP) along with their home country license. A credit card is typically required for the security deposit.

It's best to book a rental car in advance, especially during peak tourist seasons. Basic insurance is usually included, but it's advisable to check the details and consider additional coverage for extra protection. Cars are typically rented with a "full-to-full" fuel policy, meaning you must return the car with a full tank.

Driving in Italy requires awareness of local traffic laws, such as speed limits and Limited Traffic Zones (ZTL) in many city centers. Parking can be challenging in popular areas, and fines can be issued for unauthorized parking or entering restricted zones. Road conditions are generally good, but rural areas may have narrower roads.

When returning the car, make sure it's on time and in the same condition to avoid extra charges. GPS or smartphone navigation is recommended, especially in unfamiliar areas. Renting a car offers flexibility and freedom, but it's important to follow local rules and be prepared for Italy's driving environment.

 **Basic Road Rules**

When driving in Italy, it's essential to follow basic road rules to ensure your safety and avoid penalties.

- **Drive on the Right:** In Italy, you drive on the right-hand side of the road. The left lane is for overtaking (passing).

- **Speed Limits:** Adhere to speed limits:
  - 130 km/h (80.8 mph) on motorways
  - 110 km/h (68 mph) on main roads
  - 90 km/h (55.9 mph) on secondary and local roads
  - 50 km/h (31 mph) in urban areas

- **Note:** New drivers (with less than 3 years of experience) have lower speed limits, such as 100 km/h (62 mph) on motorways.

- **Seat Belts:** Seat belts are mandatory for all passengers, including those in the back seat.

- **Mobile Phones:** It's illegal to use a mobile phone while driving unless you have a hands-free system.

- **Alcohol Limits:** The legal blood alcohol limit is 0.5 grams per liter of blood. For new drivers or professional drivers, the limit is lower (0.0 grams).

- **Roundabouts:** At roundabouts, priority is generally given to vehicles coming from the right, unless there are signs indicating otherwise.

- **Pedestrian Crossings:** Always yield to pedestrians at crosswalks.

- **Traffic Signals:** Obey all traffic signs and signals. Some signs may differ from those in other countries, so be alert.

- **Parking:** Park only in designated areas. Blue lines indicate paid parking, and white lines are typically free parking (except in restricted zones). Do not park in areas marked with yellow lines or where indicated as "no parking."

- **Limited Traffic Zones (ZTL):** Many Italian cities have restricted zones (ZTL), where non-resident vehicles are not allowed to enter. Driving in these zones without permission can result in hefty fines.

- **Helmet Requirement:** Motorcyclists must wear helmets, and helmets must meet EU safety standards.

- **Toll Roads:** Many highways (autostrade) are toll roads. Have cash or a credit card ready for payment or consider getting an electronic toll device for convenience.

- **Emergency Vehicles:** Always yield to emergency vehicles (ambulances, police, fire trucks) with flashing lights and sirens. Move aside to let them pass safely.

Parking Fines

In Italy, parking fines can vary depending on the type of violation and location. Common reasons for parking fines include parking in restricted areas, exceeding time limits in paid parking zones, or parking in spaces reserved for the disabled without the appropriate permit.

Fines for illegal parking in Italy typically range from €40 (US$41.97) to €100 (US$104.93), but they can be higher in certain circumstances, especially for more serious violations or in city centers. If you park in a restricted zone, such as a *Zona Traffico Limitato* (ZTL), fines can be much steeper, sometimes over €100 (US$104.93). These fines can also be issued, if you fail to pay for parking in metered zones or park in areas with yellow lines reserved for special purposes (e.g., disabled parking spaces).

Pay attention to the color of parking lines: blue lines indicate paid parking, while white lines signify free parking. Yellow lines mark spaces that are reserved for specific purposes. Never park in spaces designated for the disabled, as these areas are clearly marked with yellow lines and often feature additional signs. Disabled parking is free for those with the proper permit, and they are also allowed to park for free in spaces marked with blue lines.

If you receive a parking ticket, it's important to pay it promptly, as fines can increase if not settled within a specified time frame. You can often pay fines online or at local post offices. If you are a foreigner, the fine will still apply, and you may be required to pay it before leaving the country.

Toll Roads and Motorways

Italy has an extensive network of toll roads, known as **autostrade**, which are major highways connecting cities, regions, and neighboring countries. These toll roads are crucial for long-distance travel and are generally in good condition, offering faster and more direct routes. The tolls are calculated based on the distance traveled, with prices varying depending on the highway and the type of vehicle.

To pay tolls, you can either use cash, credit cards, or an electronic toll device called **Telepass**, which allows for automatic payment as you drive through toll booths. There are different payment lanes: some are staffed, while others are self-service or for electronic payment only. Vehicles can also use **carpool lanes** or **motorcycle lanes** on some highways.

On motorways, the maximum speed limit is typically **130 km/h** (81 mph), though it can be lower in certain areas. **Toll fees** are collected at **toll booths**, usually at entry and exit points, and the amount depends on the distance traveled. **Heavy vehicles** like trucks or buses may face higher toll rates.

Blood Alcohol Limits in Italy

In Italy, the legal blood alcohol limit for drivers is 0.5 grams per liter, but new drivers (within the first three years) and professional drivers must maintain a 0.0 blood alcohol level.

Penalties for drunk driving vary based on blood alcohol levels. For levels up to 0.5 g/l, the offense is considered administrative, with fines ranging from €527 (US$552.98) to €6,000 (US$6,295.80). If the blood alcohol level exceeds 0.5 g/l but remains under 0.8 g/l, penalties still fall under administrative fines. However, for levels above 0.8 g/l, the offense becomes criminal, with possible fines, license suspension, and even jail time, depending on the severity of the offense.

Fines for Visiting Motorists[49]

Foreign drivers in Italy must follow the Italian Highway Code and are subject to the same penalties as Italian drivers. Italy accepts both the **Geneva Convention** (1949) and **Vienna Convention** (1968) international driving permits, provided the associated national licenses are valid. The Geneva permit is valid for one year, while the Vienna permit is valid for three years.

If caught committing a traffic offense, foreign drivers can receive a **30% discount** on fines. If the fine isn't paid on the spot, a deposit of

---

49 https://www.aci.it/fileadmin/documenti/viaggia_con_noi/pdf/ing/18__
    Fines_for_foreign_motorists.pdf

half the maximum fine must be paid, and if not paid in full, the vehicle may be seized for up to 60 days.

Italian authorities track all traffic offenses committed by foreign drivers. If a foreign driver accumulates **20 penalty points** within a year, they face a **two-year driving ban** in Italy. If accumulated within two years, the ban is one year, and within three years, it's six months.

 **General Questions**

1. *What are Italian roads like?* Italian roads are generally well-maintained, offering a mix of modern highways, narrow city streets, and scenic coastal routes. The autostrade (highways) are fast, toll-based roads connecting major cities with speed limits of up to 130 km/h (81 mph). Urban roads in older cities can be narrow and congested, with ZTL (Limited Traffic Zones) restricting access in historic areas. Rural and mountain roads are scenic but can be winding and narrow. Coastal routes, like the Amalfi Coast, offer stunning views but can be tight and steep. Overall, road conditions are good, though some rural areas may have uneven surfaces.

2. *What do the road sign colors mean?* In Italy, road signs are color-coded to convey different types of information:

> **Red:** Indicates a prohibition or restriction. For example, red circular signs typically indicate a ban, such as "No Entry" or "No Parking."
>
> **Blue:** Used for informational signs, particularly for routes and directions on highways, as well as to mark reserved parking spaces.

Green: Indicates motorways and expressways, helping to distinguish these from regular roads.

Yellow: Often used for temporary or cautionary signs, like roadworks or detours.

White: Typically used for regulatory signs that govern behavior on urban and local roads, such as speed limits or stop signs.

3. ***Is it difficult to drive in Italy as a tourist?*** Driving in Italy as a tourist offers flexibility to explore, especially in rural areas, but can be challenging in cities due to narrow streets, heavy traffic, and limited parking. Be aware of ZTL zones and parking fees. Italy also has toll roads, so factor that into your budget. Carry an International Driving Permit if needed, and follow local traffic laws to avoid fines. Overall, renting a car provides freedom, but city driving requires patience and preparation.

 **Law of the Land True Story**

A U.S. tourist learned a costly lesson about driving in Italy when he drove a Ferrari Spider into Florence's famous Piazza della Signoria, a pedestrianized area. The square, a popular spot for tourists visiting the nearby Uffizi Gallery, is not accessible to vehicles. The tourist, who was seen driving recklessly along the adjacent Via dei Gondi, was stopped by police and fined €470 (US$493.17).

Further checks revealed that his American driver's license was not compliant with international conventions, as he lacked both an international driving permit and an official translation of his license. This incident underscores the importance of understanding local driving regulations when visiting Italy. As a tourist, it's crucial to ensure your driving documents are in order to avoid fines and other legal issues.

NUDE BEACHES & CLOTHING-OPTIONAL RESORTS

NUDE BEACHES & CLOTHING-OPTIONAL RESORTS

Overview[50]

Italy boasts over 5,000 miles of Mediterranean coastline, offering some of the most stunning beaches in the world. From the dramatic cliffs of Cinque Terre to the crystal-clear waters of Sardinia, Italy's shores are a popular destination for sunbathers and those seeking picturesque ocean views.

Among these coastal gems, a few beaches are dedicated to naturism, allowing visitors to enjoy the freedom of sunbathing nude. While nudist beaches can be a controversial topic, they offer a unique opportunity for those looking to relax without swimsuits or social barriers.

Italy has a long history of naturism, with the first official nude beach opening at Lido di Dante on the Adriatic Sea in 1890. Initially marketed as a health-focused destination for sunbathing, the practice of nude beach-going spread across Italy, with many nudist camps and beach colonies emerging by the 1920s. Today, Italy offers several stunning locations for nude sunbathing, including Sardinia's Spiaggia della Pelosa, Liguria's Spiaggia di Guvano, Tuscany's Baratti and Marcello beaches,

---

50 https://medium.com/@italybestplaces/
    nude-beaches-of-italy-2ab77e576260

the Amalfi Coast, and Sicily's Piana Grande de la Pelosa, each offering picturesque, secluded settings for naturists.

In Italy, attitudes toward nudity are generally more liberal than in many other Western countries. Topless sunbathing is widely accepted on most beaches, and specific areas are designated for those who prefer to sunbathe completely nude. Although the number of official nude beaches is relatively small, their historical significance and scenic settings make them appealing to open-minded travelers. However, with some politicians advocating for a ban on nude sunbathing, the future of these clothing-optional spots remains uncertain.

 ## Nude Beach Regulation

In Italy, most nude beaches are not officially sanctioned but operate under a general acceptance of nudity. Topless sunbathing is widely tolerated, but full nudity is restricted to designated zones, which are usually located at the ends of beaches for privacy. Visitors must adhere to the boundaries of these clothing-optional sections to avoid potential fines or confrontations.

Nudist areas are generally secluded, and behaviors like photography or gawking are prohibited. The spaces are intended for relaxation, not exhibitionism. Additionally, wandering into clothed sections or nearby towns in the nude is not allowed.

In recent years, there have been attempts to ban nudity on Italian beaches, with some local ordinances and a proposed national bill seeking to impose fines for public nudity. While these efforts have not yet succeeded, they highlight ongoing challenges for Italy's nude beach culture. Despite this, many nude beaches continue to thrive, either through tradition or unofficial recognition, offering visitors a chance to embrace naturism in stunning coastal settings. However, with increasing development and opposition to public nudity, the future of these beaches is uncertain. Those wishing to experience Italy's nude beaches are advised to act soon, while respecting local rules and etiquette.

Best Nude Beaches in Italy[51]

Italy's Mediterranean coastline offers some of Europe's most beautiful nude-friendly beaches. From secluded spots in Sardinia to serene coves in Sicily, the country has a variety of locations where naturism is welcomed. Here's a guide to some of the best nude beaches in Italy, perfect for those seeking a liberating beach experience.

- **Capocotta Beach, Lazio:** Capocotta, officially recognized as Italy's first nudist beach in 2000, is a naturist haven in Ostia, Lazio. The beach is nestled within a protected nature reserve, surrounded by white sand dunes and lush Mediterranean flora.

- **Troncone Beach, Campania:** Located in Marina di Camerota within the Cilento National Park, Troncone Beach became a naturist-friendly spot in 2011, making it a popular destination for naturists in Southern Italy.

- **Punta del Miglio, Tuscany:** South of Livorno, Punta del Miglio is a small, scenic cove known for its naturist-friendly atmosphere, especially popular among LGBTQI+ travelers. This designated nude-friendly beach is well-marked and welcoming.

- **Acquarilli Beach, Elba Island:** Elba Island, known for its numerous beaches, boasts Acquarilli Beach as one of its most famous naturist spots. Situated in the Municipality of Capolivieri, it is a favorite among naturism enthusiasts.

- **San Saba Beach, Sicily:** San Saba, officially recognized in 2022 as a naturist beach, offers a peaceful and secluded escape just 25 km (15.5 miles) from Messina. It's considered one of the most beautiful beaches in the region.

---

51 https://www.ferryhopper.com/en/blog/featured/top-nude-friendly-beaches-italy

- **Cala Cottone, Pantelleria:** Accessible by ferry from Trapani, Pantelleria is home to Cala Cottone, a nude-friendly beach in a stunning location. Nudism is common on many beaches here, including its thermal pools.

- **Fiorenzuola di Focara, Marche:** Located within the Monte San Bartolo Nature Park near Pesaro, Fiorenzuola di Focara is a popular clothing-optional beach. Its peaceful, semi-deserted charm makes it a favorite naturist retreat.

- **Costa dei Barbari, Friuli-Venezia Giulia:** In northeastern Italy, Costa dei Barbari near Trieste is a pristine, rocky bay where naturism is well-accepted. Its clean waters and natural beauty offer a perfect place to connect with nature.

- **Vignanotica Beach, Puglia:** Situated in the Gargano region near Vieste, Vignanotica is a pebble beach surrounded by high cliffs and caves. Its natural setting makes it an excellent choice for those seeking a quiet, naturist-friendly spot.

- **Razza di Junco Beach, Sardinia:** Just 18 km (11 miles) from Olbia, Razza di Junco in Costa Smeralda is a paradise for both clothed and nude bathers. It's a stunning beach, where you can enjoy the breathtaking beauty of the coast, with or without a swimsuit.

 Important: Be cautious when choosing to go nude on public, crowded beaches in Italy, as you may face fines of up to €1,200 (US$1,259.16).

Nude Beach Etiquette

When visiting a nudist beach in Italy, it's essential to be respectful and follow basic etiquette. For example, it's customary to bring a towel to sit on and avoid taking photos or videos without permission from others around you. Additionally, not all visitors may feel comfortable with physical contact or nudity beyond the designated areas, so it's important to be mindful of others' boundaries.

Legally, while nudity is permitted on official nudist beaches, it is still governed by the same rules as other public spaces. Inappropriate behavior, such as public sexual acts, can lead to legal consequences.

In short, although public nudity is regulated in Italy, there are designated areas where you can enjoy being nude. By respecting the beach's etiquette and being aware of local laws, your visit to a nudist beach can be an enjoyable and memorable experience.

 **General Questions**

1. ***What is a topless beach?*** A topless beach is a beach where sunbathers are permitted to go without wearing a bikini top or shirt, while still remaining covered from the waist down with swimwear. Topless sunbathing is generally allowed in certain areas and is often tolerated or encouraged on beaches that are more liberal about nudity, but it doesn't mean that full nudity is allowed. Most beaches in Italy are topless beaches.

2. ***What is a nude beach?*** A nude beach is a beach where visitors are allowed to be fully nude. It caters to those who want to enjoy the natural experience of sunbathing or swimming without swimwear. These beaches are often part of the naturist or nudist movement, promoting body acceptance and a connection with nature.

   While some nude beaches are officially designated, others are informally accepted. It's important to follow proper etiquette and rules, as inappropriate behavior like exhibitionism or voyeurism is typically prohibited. Respect for others and the designated nude zones is key when visiting.

3. ***Can you take photos on a nude beach?*** Generally, photography on nude beaches is discouraged or outright prohibited to respect people's privacy and comfort. Since these beaches attract individuals who prefer to relax in the nude, many visitors expect a certain level of discretion and respect for personal boundaries.

In many cases, signs will indicate whether photography is allowed or not. Even if photography is permitted, it is always important to get explicit consent from people before taking their photos. Inappropriate or intrusive behavior, such as photographing others without permission, can lead to legal consequences and cause discomfort among other beachgoers.

 **Law of the Land Hypothetical**

HYPOTHETICAL: *Tom and his partner are on vacation in Italy and decide to visit a nude beach on the island of Sardinia. They're new to naturism and want to make sure they respect local customs. They wonder if there are any specific rules or behaviors they should be aware of while enjoying the beach.*

ANSWER: *Tom and his partner should be aware that, while nude beaches in Italy are welcoming, it's important to respect the norms. They should always use a towel to sit on and avoid walking around the beach in the nude, unless they are in the designated nude area. Public displays of affection or inappropriate behavior are not acceptable and could lead to legal consequences. They should also avoid taking photos of others without consent, as this can be seen as invasive. As long as they respect the local etiquette and enjoy the beach in a relaxed and respectful way, they should have a wonderful experience.*

UNUSUAL LAWS

UNUSUAL LAWS

Unusual Laws in Italy[52]

Italy is known for its rich culture, history, and vibrant cities, but it's also home to some strange and unique laws. Here are a few quirky regulations you might want to be aware of when visiting:

- **No Sandcastles in Eraclea:** Building sandcastles is banned in this small beach town near Venice, with fines ranging from €25 (US$26.23) to €250 (US$262.32).

- **No Round Goldfish Bowls in Rome:** A law passed in 2011 prohibits round goldfish bowls, as they're considered cruel to fish, with the shape not providing enough oxygen.

- **No Feeding the Birds in Venice:** Once a popular tourist activity, feeding pigeons in Venice is now illegal, with fines of up to €700 (US$734.51).

- **No Public Genital Adjustments:** In 2008, Italy's Supreme Court ruled that adjusting your genitals in public is a criminal offense, regardless of the reason.

- **No Noisy Footwear on Capri:** Wearing noisy sandals or clogs on Capri can lead to fines or even arrest, as loud footwear is strictly prohibited.

---

52 https://www.ecnews.it/wp-content/uploads/pdf/2023-05-17_10-of-the-strangest-laws-from-italy.pdf

- **No Groups of Three After 11 p.m. in Novara:** In Novara, it's illegal to sit on a park bench in groups of three after 11 p.m., and fines may follow if caught.

- **No Eating on the Streets in Florence:** In Florence, eating on the street is banned during certain hours (noon to 3 p.m. and 6 p.m. to 10 p.m.), with fines up to €500 (US$524.65) for violations.

- **Dogs Must Be Walked in Turin:** Dog owners in Turin are required to walk their dogs at least three times a day or face fines.

Do's and Don'ts While in Italy

Navigating social norms and cultural expectations can be tricky, even at home. When traveling to a new country, understanding local etiquette becomes even more crucial. To help you avoid common pitfalls and blend in more seamlessly, here are some helpful "Do's and Don'ts" for your trip to Italy.

Do's

- **Be Mindful of How You Dress:** Italians care about fashion, and how you present yourself matters. Avoid the stereotypical tourist look (e.g., flip-flops or overly casual clothing). Aim for a polished and stylish appearance.

- **Remember to Cover Your Knees and Shoulders:** When visiting churches or religious sites, such as St. Peter's Basilica or St. Mark's Basilica, ensure your knees and shoulders are covered. Modest dress is required for entry.

- **Use Formal Greetings:** When meeting someone for the first time, say "Buon Giorno" (good morning) or "Buona Sera" (good afternoon/evening) instead of "Ciao." Italians appreciate it when you make an effort to speak their language, even if it's just a few words.

- **Carry Some Cash:** Not all establishments accept credit cards, so it's important to carry cash with you. This ensures you're never caught without a way to pay for smaller purchases or meals.

Don'ts

- **Don't Rush Your Meal:** Italians take their time when eating, especially during long, leisurely meals. Don't rush through your meal, as dining is a social and cultural event. Allow the courses to come at a comfortable pace.

- **Don't Overlook Local Etiquette:** Italians appreciate politeness and social decorum. Make sure to follow local customs, such as waiting for your host to begin a meal or offering a friendly greeting to others.

- **Don't Expect Restaurants to Serve Tap Water Automatically:** Unlike in many countries, tap water is not typically served unless you ask for it. Be prepared to order "acqua del rubinetto" (tap water) if you want it, or opt for bottled water, which is more common.

- **Don't Tip Too Much:** Tipping is appreciated but not expected in Italy. A small tip (around 5-10%) is enough, and some restaurants may include a "coperto" (cover charge), which is a fixed fee for bread and service. Check your bill before leaving extra.

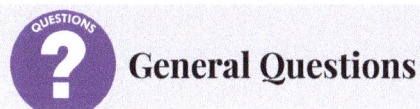 **General Questions**

1. *Is it legal to swim in Venice's canals?* **No**, swimming in Venice's canals is illegal due to safety, pollution, and preservation concerns. The water can be hazardous, and it disrupts boat traffic. Violators can face fines. For swimming, it's best to head to nearby beaches like those in the Lido district.

2. *Can I cool off by getting in a fountain in Rome?* **No**, jumping into fountains in Rome is illegal. Many of the city's iconic fountains, including the Trevi Fountain, are protected as historical monuments. Swimming, climbing, or entering them is prohibited, and violators can face hefty fines. It's best to admire these beautiful landmarks from a distance!

3. *Can I sit on the Spanish Steps in Rome?* **No**, sitting on the Spanish Steps in Rome is prohibited. In 2019, the city imposed a ban on sitting on the steps to preserve the historic site and manage overcrowding. The fine for sitting on the steps can be up to €400 (US$419.72). Visitors are encouraged to admire the steps from the surrounding areas, but sitting on them is no longer allowed.

 **Law of the Land True Story**[53]

Two backpackers were recently fined €900 (US$997.56) in Venice for brewing coffee at the foot of the Rialto Bridge. The pair set up a camping stove early in the morning, drawing the ire of locals who found the activity disrespectful in such a historic location. The Rialto Bridge, one of Venice's most iconic landmarks, attracts thousands of tourists, and local laws prohibit cooking or engaging in activities that could damage the environment or the city's heritage.

The incident led to a call to the police, who issued the fine for violating public space regulations. This case highlights the growing tensions between tourists and locals, as Venice tightens enforcement to protect its cultural and historical sites. The fine serves as a reminder of the city's strict rules and the importance of respecting its public spaces.

---

53 https://www.thelocal. it/20190819/15-strange-ways-to-get-into-trouble-on-holiday-in-italy

TRAVELING SAFELY

TRAVELING SAFELY

 **Safety Tips While Traveling in Italy**[54]

Italy is a beautiful and welcoming country, but like any popular tourist destination, it's important to stay aware of your surroundings and take basic precautions to stay safe. While most travelers enjoy trouble-free visits, being mindful of common risks—such as pickpocketing, scams, and theft—can help you avoid unpleasant situations. Staying safe requires a combination of preparation, awareness, and common sense. By following basic safety tips and staying alert, you can enjoy a safe and memorable trip to Italy.

Here are some key safety tips to keep in mind while in Italy:

Keep Valuables Secure: Use a money belt or hidden pouch for passports, wallets, and phones, and avoid carrying large amounts of cash. Be cautious in crowded areas like tourist attractions, markets, and public transport.

---

54 https://tinyurl.com/4xxt5z99

Beware of Pickpockets: In busy areas, especially on public transport and at popular tourist sites (like the Colosseum or Vatican), keep bags close to your body, and avoid having items visible.

Avoid Scams: Be cautious of street vendors offering unsolicited help, and beware of "free" gifts or services, which may lead to aggressive requests for money. Stick to reputable services and vendors.

Secure Accommodation: Lock doors and windows in your hotel or rental, and use hotel safes for valuables. Never leave items unattended in your room or common areas.

Watch Food and Drinks: Don't leave drinks or food unattended in public spaces, and be wary of accepting drinks from strangers, as tampering with food and beverages is a risk.

Stay Alert in Traffic: If you're driving, park in well-lit, secure areas and keep valuables out of sight. Watch out for scams, such as staged accidents, and always lock your car doors.

Monitor Strikes and Protests: Strikes or demonstrations can disrupt public transportation or services. Check local news, and avoid participating in large gatherings.

Know Emergency Numbers: The emergency number for police, medical, and fire services in Italy is 112. Keep contact details for your embassy or consulate handy in case of emergencies.

Protect Your Personal Info: Avoid using public Wi-Fi for financial transactions, and cover your PIN when using ATMs to prevent card skimming.

Follow Local Laws and Customs: Understand Italian customs, especially regarding dress codes for religious sites, local alcohol regulations, and public behavior.

? General Questions

1. ***Is Italy safe?*** Italy is generally safe for travelers, but petty crime like pickpocketing and bag snatching is common in crowded tourist areas. Remain vigilant, especially in big cities like Rome, Milan, and Naples.[55]

2. ***Do I need to carry cash in Italy?*** In Italy, you don't need to carry large amounts of cash. While cash is required for smaller purchases at cafes and shops, most other transactions can be made with a credit or debit card. It's recommended to carry no more than €50 (US$52.46) - €100 (US$104.93) in cash at any given time. Bring two cards—your primary one and a backup for emergencies. Leave your main wallet and unnecessary cards at home, and consider using a smaller wallet with RFID protection (Radio-frequency Identification Wallet Protection) to guard against electronic pickpocketing.

3. ***Do I need to carry an ID while traveling in Italy?*** **Yes**, it is required to carry official identification while traveling in Italy. For non-Europeans, this means carrying your passport. A U.S. driver's license is not considered an official form of ID in Italy. It's a good idea to have a photocopy of your passport with you as well, in case the original is lost or stolen, but always keep the original in a safe place.

---

55 https://www.untoldmorsels.com/how-to-avoid-pickpockets-in-italy/

 **Law of the Land Hypothetical**

HYPOTHETICAL: *Samantha, a tourist from the United States, is visiting Rome for the first time. She's excited to see the Colosseum, but while walking through the crowded Piazza del Colosseo, she feels a sudden bump from behind. She turns around and notices a man quickly walking away. When she checks her bag, she realizes her wallet is missing. What should Samantha have done differently to prevent this situation, and what should she do now that her wallet has been stolen?*

ANSWER: *To prevent this, Samantha should have kept her bag in front of her in crowded areas, used a crossbody bag with zippers, and kept her valuables in a money belt or neck pouch.*

Now that her wallet has been stolen, Samantha should immediately report the theft to local authorities. In Italy, police can issue a report that may be necessary for insurance claims or if she needs to cancel any stolen credit cards. She should also contact her bank or credit card companies to freeze her accounts and prevent unauthorized transactions. Lastly, if she is staying in a hotel, Samantha should inform the staff and check if they have any security tips for recovering stolen items in the area.

CHAPTER 22

TOURIST TAXATION

CHAPTER 22

TOURIST TAXATION

Overview[56]

Tourist taxation in Italy includes several types of taxes that visitors may encounter during their stay. The most common is the **tourism tax**, or *Tassa di Soggiorno*, which is a local tax imposed by many cities and municipalities on overnight stays at accommodations like hotels, B&Bs, and guesthouses. This tax varies by location, accommodation type, and the number of stars a property has.

Additionally, tourists will pay **Value Added Tax** (**VAT**), known locally as *IVA*, which is included in the price of most goods and services, such as meals, transportation, and accommodations. In some cities, visitors may also face entry fees to museums, cultural sites, or other attractions, which help maintain Italy's rich historical and cultural heritage. These taxes are generally paid directly to accommodations or businesses and are an important aspect of travel costs in Italy.

While not technically a tourist tax, **airport taxes** are included in the price of your airline ticket, covering services and infrastructure at airports. This tax is often included in your flight cost and is not something tourists typically pay separately at the airport.

---

56   https://expertoitaly.com/italian-tourist-tax-what-is-it-and-how-much

Additionally, in some cities or cultural attractions, visitors may pay **Cultural Heritage Tax**, which is an additional fee for entry to museums, historical sites, or cultural institutions. These fees are often used to maintain Italy's extensive cultural and historical heritage.

How Tourist Tax is Determined

The tourist tax is assessed on a per-night, per-guest basis, and the rate can vary significantly due to several factors:

- **Destination:** Each municipality in Italy sets its own tax rates. Popular tourist cities like Rome, Venice, and Florence generally have higher rates due to their high volumes of visitors.

- **Type of Accommodation:** The rate can differ depending on the type and accommodation category. For example, a 5-star hotel will have a higher tax rate than a B&B or a hostel.

- **Season:** Some locations adjust their rates based on the time of year, with higher taxes during peak tourist seasons.

 You can calculate tourist tax at **https://www.visitbergamo.net/en/tourist-tax-pro/ calculator/**.

? General Questions

1. *Are any visitors exempt from tourist tax?* Some tourists may be exempt from tourist taxes, depending on local rules. Common exemptions include tourists with disabilities (and their companions), children, short stays, and residents of the area. Additionally, diplomats or those on official business may also be

exempt. Exemption criteria vary by location, so it's best to check specific regulations before traveling.

2. ***When do you pay?*** Most owners or property managers collect the tourist tax from guests upon checking out.

3. ***Whut huppens if you do not pay/pay incorrectly?*** Local au thorities actively monitor the payment of tourist taxes to ensure compliance, and evading payment is not an option. Those who pay an incorrect amount or fail to pay altogether may face penalties, including having to pay double the standard tax amount.

 ## Law of the Land Hypothetical

HYPOTHETICAL: *If Mr. and Mrs. Pool stayed at a 5-star hotel in Venice, at a rate of US$700 per night for five nights, and were accompanied by their two children, ages 15 and 16, what would the total tourist tax be?*

ANSWER:

-*Hotel rate: US$700 per night*

-*Tourist tax: €5.00 (US$5.56) per person per night*

-*Total number of guests: 4 (2 adults, 2 children)*

-*Number of nights: 5*

Tourist tax calculation:

€5.00 (US$5) per person × 4 guests = €20 ($20.99) per night

€20.00 (US$20.99) per night × 5 nights = €100.00 ($104.93) total tourist tax

LONG-TERM STAYS

CHAPTER 23

LONG-TERM STAYS

Overview[57]

Foreigners are drawn to Italy for long-term stays for a variety of reasons, from cultural immersion to lifestyle benefits. One of the biggest appeals is Italy's rich cultural heritage. The country is home to world-renowned art, history, and architecture, with landmarks like the Colosseum, the Leaning Tower of Pisa, and Renaissance treasures in Florence.

Italy's lifestyle is another major draw — from food and wine to a strong focus on work-life balance and family. The slower pace, especially in regions like Tuscany and Sicily, is attractive to many, particularly retirees. The mild climate, beautiful landscapes, and affordable healthcare make Italy a popular choice for those seeking a peaceful retirement abroad.

Professional opportunities in Italy are also appealing. The country is a global hub for industries like fashion, automotive design, and cuisine. Cities like Milan and Rome offer career prospects, while many "digital nomads" find Italy's welcoming atmosphere and high-quality infrastructure ideal for remote work. Students are also attracted to Italy's prestigious universities and renowned academic programs, which allow them to study in a culturally rich environment.

---

57   https://tinyurl.com/mfdne3tc

For many, the allure of Italian cuisine and wine is undeniable. Italy's culinary tradition, with its emphasis on fresh, local ingredients and regional specialties, makes it a paradise for food lovers. Living in Italy offers the chance to enjoy some of the best food and wine in the world on a daily basis.

Lastly, Italy's visa options make it easier for foreigners to live there long-term. From the *Elective Residence Visa* for retirees to student and work visas, there are various avenues to gain residency, making it relatively simple for foreigners to settle in the country.

Temporary Residency Permit for Non-EU Citizens

Non-EU citizens, who wish to stay in Italy for more than 90 days, must obtain a national long-stay visa (Type D) and a residence permit.

Visa Application (Type D)

Non-EU citizens are required to apply for a Type D visa at an Italian consulate or embassy in their home country before traveling to Italy. The visa is valid only for the period indicated on the application.

Applicants must provide documentation that may include employment verification, such as a letter from their employer stating their position, salary, and approved vacation or leave. Self-employed applicants need to submit a business license, certificate of incorporation, and their most recent tax return. Students must provide a full-time enrollment letter, and, in some cases, a valid I-20 Form, or an IAP-66 Form for exchange visitors. Applicants must also provide proof of health insurance that covers medical expenses, hospitalization, and repatriation for at least €30,000 (US$31,479) during their stay. Additionally, applicants are required to state the purpose of their visit, their means of transportation and return, their financial support during the trip, and details about their accommodation arrangements.

Temporary Residence Permit

After arriving in Italy, non-EU citizens intending to stay for more than 90 days must apply for a temporary residence permit within eight days. This application can only be made once the applicant holds a valid Type D visa, such as a work, student, self-employment, family reunion, elective residence, or golden visa.

The application process involves two steps: first, visiting the local police station (*Questura*) to complete a residence declaration and provide fingerprints. Next, the applicant must go to a local post office (*Patronato*) to submit additional forms known as "The Kit," which are required to schedule an appointment at the police station. This appointment is typically set about 60 days after submitting the kit, but it may take up to six months.

Required documents include four passport-sized photos, a valid passport, proof of the purpose of stay (e.g., employment contract or school enrollment), all documents submitted for the visa, and proof of private health insurance. Applicants must bring both original documents and photocopies.

Processing Time and Costs of Residency Permit

Visa application processing typically takes one to three months from the time the application is submitted. However, this can vary depending on the embassy or consulate and the type of visa being applied for. The entire process, from initial application to obtaining residency status, can take nine to 12 months.

Cost

1. **Visa Application Fee:** Generally around €120 (US$125.92) (can vary based on visa type and embassy).

2. **Permesso di Soggiorno (residence permit):** Costs range from €80 (US$83.94) to €130 (US$136.44).

3. **Residence Card:** Typically about €30 (US$31.49).

4. **Additional Handling Fees:** Around €45 (US$47.23).

5. **Immigration Attorney or Consultant Fees:** If you choose to hire professional assistance, expect to pay between €1,000 (US$1,049.50) and €5,000 (US$5,247.50). Additional fees for translation and apostille services may also apply.

Validity

The validity of your Italian residence permit depends on the purpose of your stay in the country. The most common types of residence permits and their corresponding validity are as follows:

PURPOSE OF RESIDENCE PERMIT	VALIDITY
Academic	1 year
Seasonal work	6 to 9 months
Regular employment	Up to 2 years
Family reunification	2 years

Renewing Your Residence Permit

The renewal timelines for your Italian residence permit are as follows: For permits valid up to six months, you must apply for renewal at least 30 days before the expiration date. For permits valid for one or two years, renewal must be initiated at least 90 days before the expiration date.

For your extension appointment, you'll need to bring the same documents as you did for your initial application. You can submit your extension request at the local post office, trade unions, or the municipality.

The cost of the renewal depends on the type of residence permit, with prices starting at €80 (US$83.96).

 **Penalties for Overstaying & Non-Compliance**

The maximum stay of 90 days cannot be extended, except in cases of force majeure (such as a natural disaster or other uncontrollable circumstances). Foreigners who enter or remain in Italy in violation of immigration regulations can face a fine ranging from €5,000 (US$5,247.50) to €10,000 (US$10,495).[58]

 **General Questions**

1. *What happens if I overstay while in Italy?* If you are caught overstaying in Italy by the police (outside of border checks), the authorities will treat it as a criminal offense. They will first verify your identity using your passport, and then initiate legal proceedings for a misdemeanor, which may result in a fine.

2. *How is Italy enforcing the 90-day limit?* Among EU countries, Italy is known for being relatively lenient, and deportations are uncommon for individuals who are not working or receiving benefits—unless they have lived in Italy for many years without the proper documentation.

---

58 https://www.smartdualcitizenship.com/blog/what-happens-if-you-over-stay-in-italy-and-europe/#:~:text=In%20Italy%2C%20overstaying%20is%20considered,286).

 **Law of the Land Hypothetical**

HYPOTHETICAL: *John, a Canadian citizen, arrives in Italy on a short-term tourist visa. He initially planned to stay for three weeks but decides to extend his stay for another six months due to personal reasons. However, he doesn't apply for a residence permit or extension and continues staying beyond the 90-day limit. He becomes concerned when he realizes that overstaying his visa could lead to fines or even deportation. Is there any way to resolve John's situation without facing penalties?"*

ANSWER: **Yes**. *If John acts quickly and seeks legal advice, there may be a chance to resolve the situation before it escalates. For example, he could apply for a permit to stay for humanitarian reasons or show the authorities that he's making an effort to comply with immigration rules. However, there's no guarantee that he will avoid penalties.*

CIVIL LITIGATION

CIVIL LITIGATION

Overview

The Italian legal process for civil litigation typically involves four main stages. **Introduction**, allows all parties to present their respective legal positions. **Treatment**, parties provide arguments and legal precedents to support or defend their positions. **Exhibition of Proof**, gives parties the opportunity to present evidence to substantiate their claims or defenses. Finally, in the **Court Decision** stage, the court issues a ruling based on the legal positions, arguments, precedents, and evidence presented.

The entire process, from Introduction to Court decision, can take several years. Additionally, Italy's legal system has three levels of judicial review. After the court's decision, many cases are appealed to the *Corte d'Appello* (Appellate Court) and, in some instances, to the *Corte di Cassazione* (the highest appellate court).

 Civil Litigation Process

Legal representation is mandatory in most civil proceedings in Italy, with a few exceptions. Legal representation is not required for disputes handled by the *giudice di pace* (a judge of first instance) for cases involving lower-value claims (up to €10,000 (US$10,495) or €25,000 (US$26,237.50), depending on the subject matter) or in certain other specific disputes. Additionally, legal representation is not required if the amount in dispute is less than €1,100 (US$1,154.45), or if the giudice di pace authorizes a party to proceed without an attorney due to the nature or amount of the case.

In Italy, civil proceedings begin with the claimant serving a writ of summons. The first hearing is scheduled at least 120 days later. Before the hearing, parties must submit additional evidence and claims. The judge may seek settlement, review evidence, and schedule further hearings if needed.

After the evidence phase, a final hearing occurs within 1-2 years, and the judge issues a decision within 60 days. The decision is enforceable even if appealed. The losing party generally pays legal costs, and in cases of bad faith, may face fines or additional damages.

Statute of Limitations

In Italy, the statute of limitations sets a deadline for bringing legal claims, after which the right to pursue the claim is lost. Key limitation periods include:

- **Contract claims:** 10 years, starting from when the right could have been enforced.
- **Tort claims (e.g., personal injury or damage):** 5 years, starting from the event or when the damage is discovered.
- **Property rights claims:** 20 years, starting when the claimant could assert their rights.
- **Inheritance claims:** 10 years, starting from the opening of the succession (death).
- **Personal injury claims:** 5 years, starting from when the injury occurs or is discovered.

Certain actions can interrupt or suspend the statute of limitations, such as filing a lawsuit or negotiating a settlement.

Discovery under Italian Law

There is no obligation of discovery under Italian law, which means that the parties are not obliged to share relevant documents unless an order to this effect is issued by a judge. Such orders can only be made when a party specifically requests a document to be disclosed and the judge deems such disclosure necessary. A party receiving a document request is not obliged to disclose the document requested. In practice, disclosure only occurs when the documents requested do not harm the disclosing party's case.

Cost of Litigation

Court fees depend on the value of the dispute and the stage of the case (first instance, appeal, or Supreme Court). They typically range from €40 (US$41.98) to €4,000 (US$4,198).

The losing party in a civil case is typically ordered to pay the legal costs of the winning party, including attorneys' fees. The amount is determined by the court and usually covers only a portion of the actual legal costs incurred.

If the losing party has acted with gross negligence or bad faith during the proceedings, the winning party may be entitled to claim damages for the harm caused, as well as a fine ranging from €500 (US$524.75) to €5,000 (US$5,247.50), under Article 96 of the Italian Civil Code. Generally, Italian law does not award punitive damages.[59]

---

59 https://www.dlapiperintelligence.com/litigation/insight/

? General Questions

1. *In what language(s) are court proceedings in Italy conducted?*
Court proceedings are conducted in Italian.

2. *What if I don't speak Italian?* Non-Italian citizens involved in
legal proceedings in Italy have the right to a court-appointed
interpreter to ensure they understand the language of the trial
and the documents presented. The court will appoint a sworn
translator, who must take an oath before performing their duties.
Additionally, any documents submitted in a foreign language
must be translated into Italian by a certified translator.

Law of the Land True Story

Lidia Poët's story marks a pivotal moment in Italy's legal history, high-
lighting the intersection of gender, law, and social progress. A trailblaz-
er for women in law, Poët graduated from the University of Turin in
1881 and was admitted to the bar in 1883, defying the male-dominated
legal establishment. However, just three months into her practice, she
was disbarred by the attorney general, who argued that women had no
place in the courtroom.

Though her career was abruptly halted, the case sparked a nationwide
debate on gender equality, ultimately leading to her readmission to the
bar in 1920 at the age of 65.

CHAPTER 25

OTHER THINGS TO KNOW

OTHER THINGS TO KNOW

When you are visiting a new and exciting place like Italy, you want to be able to enjoy yourself and have the most amazing time possible.

Below are some things to keep in mind while visiting Italy.

 ## Cultural Etiquette for Tourists

- A firm handshake with direct eye contact for new acquaintances, while close friends and family typically greet with kisses on both cheeks.

- Standing up when an older person enters a room, opening doors for them, and addressing them with titles like "Signore" or "Signora."

- Waiting for the host to start eating, keeping hands visible on the table, and not rushing to leave after a meal because dining is seen as a social event.

- Dressing neatly and appropriately for the situation.

- Italians tend to stand closer to each other during conversation and may use light touches to convey friendliness.

- While it's best to be on time for appointments, social gatherings can often start a bit later than the stated time.

Getting Around in Italy

- Renting a car is the best option to get around in Italy as there are almost no taxis outside of big cities.

- The center of the big cities is a "limited traffic area." If you rent a car in Italy, be sure not to drive past a ZTL (zona a traffico limitato) sign, as doing so will result in a fine.

- **Parking:** White lines indicate free parking, blue lines mean you need to pay, and yellow lines signify no parking allowed. However, there are exceptions, such as in the center of Florence, where white lines are reserved for residents only.

- To hail a taxi in Italy, you need to call one, book it via an app, or go to a designated taxi rank to reserve one. Taxis generally can't be flagged down on the street. Additionally, many taxis do not accept credit cards.

Food Etiquette in Italy

- For Italians, cappuccino is a morning drink, but they drink espresso all day long.

- If you order a "latte," you'll be served milk. The correct term for a coffee with milk is "caffè latte."

- Restaurants close at 3 p.m. after lunch and open again around 7 p.m. for dinner. In the meantime, you can eat in a bar or get some street food to tie you over.

- "Coperto" is a charge applied to each person dining at a restaurant, typically just a few euros. Some restaurants charge it, while others don't. This is separate from tips, which are not obligatory in Italy.

- Italians don't eat bread with pasta. Italians are typically very mindful of the balance of carbs in their diet, as part of the renowned Mediterranean diet they take great pride in. While it's common to use bread to scoop up the last bits of food on your plate, it's not something you'd typically do in a restaurant, especially a fine dining establishment.

- If you want to find good authentic food, try the streets away from the main touristic places and see where the locals go.

- Pizza in Italy varies by region. In Rome, the dough is made with olive oil and is thinner than in Naples. If you order a "pepperoni" pizza, you'll receive one with red peppers, not salami. Also, avoid ordering Hawaiian pizza—Italians are generally quite offended by it across the country.

- In Italy, you'll need to ask for the bill when you're ready to leave. Italians often enjoy lingering and chatting after a meal, so the check is not typically brought to you right away.

- You can only find Starbucks in Milan and Turin, otherwise Italians prefer their local coffee bars.

Other Things to Know

- Not everyone speaks English, especially outside of the main tourist areas, so learning Italian phrases might be extremely useful.

- Train travel is inexpensive and can take you almost anywhere in Italy. However, remember to validate your ticket.

- Public restrooms are rare in Italy, and you may need to pay to use them. It's a good idea to use the bathroom before you leave your accommodation or in the restaurant after a meal.

- In Rome, you can drink from the public fountains, which are typically old-fashioned spouts that provide a continuous stream of cold, fresh water.

- Italy is known for its aperitivo, a pre-dinner tradition usually in the early evening, where you enjoy a drink with light snacks or appetizers. In some places, a buffet is included with the drink.

Practical Tips

- Your passport must be valid for at least six more months to travel to Italy, otherwise the airline might not allow you to board.

- Don't change money at the airport as the exchange rates are usually not favorable. It's better to withdraw money from an ATM, which will get you the best rate.

- Generally, the daily limit for cash withdrawals is €250 (US$262.38) per day. Before traveling, make sure your bank doesn't have any international restrictions on withdrawals. When paying with your card, specify you want to pay in euros.

- Italy uses a European two-pin plug, so don't forget a converter for your devices.

- **Italy uses three types of plugs:** type C (two round pins), type F (two round pins with two earth clips on the sides), and type L (three round pins). The country operates on a 230V supply voltage and 50Hz frequency.

- In smaller cities and the countryside, shops and services typically close for a lunch break from between1 to 4 p.m., so plan accordingly.

In the Event of Death[60]

 While the information included below is specific to U.S. citizens, the majority of other countries follow similar guidelines.

When repatriating remains from Italy to the U.S., the next of kin must first contact the American Citizen Services (ACS) office in the consular district where the death occurred. They will help prepare the Consular Report of Death and guide the family through local procedures, such as assisting in finding a funeral agent in Italy.

A death certificate from the hospital or doctor is required, which the funeral agent will help obtain from local authorities. The repatriation process typically takes four to seven days, though burial in Italy can happen within 48 hours. Embalming is usually unavailable in Italy unless

---

60 https://it.usembassy.gov/u-s-citizen-services/death-of-a-u-s-citizen/

for international transport, and an autopsy is generally required. For cremation, the next of kin must authorize the process, and the ACS will issue the necessary statement. There can be delays of several weeks in obtaining ashes from the crematorium.

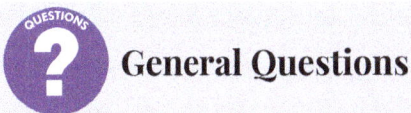

General Questions

1. ***What city was Italy's first capital?*** Turin became the first capital in 1861, when Victor Emmanuel II of Savoy was proclaimed the first King of Italy. Florence was the second Italian capital city from 1865 to 1870, and Rome has been the capital since 1871.

2. ***What wine do Italians pair with fish?*** White wine is the preferred choice to pair with fish dishes due to its lighter, more delicate nature. Fish typically has mild flavors that could be overpowered by a full-bodied red wine, while white wine enhances these flavors without overwhelming them.

3. ***What does "ciao" mean?*** Ciao means both "hello" and "goodbye." It is used in informal settings, generally among family members and friends. The modern word derives from the 18th-century Venetian dialect, where the phrase s-ciào vostro meant "I am your slave."

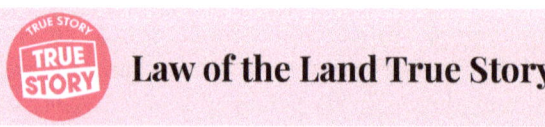

Law of the Land True Story

The modern aperitivo (a beverage) originated in Piedmont, specifically in Turin, one of Italy's most renowned regions. In 1786, Antonio Benedetto Carpano, a traditional distiller, grew bored with his usual work and began experimenting in his lab. By chance, he combined aromatic herbs and ingredients such as vanilla, saffron, and wormwood, creating Vermouth. The drink quickly gained popularity in the region, offering a new bittersweet flavor that appealed to locals without being overly expensive.[61]

Embassy Contact Information

The main purpose of embassies in Italy is to represent their respective countries, promoting their interests and providing support and protection to their citizens while they are in Italy. Rome, Italy's capital, is home to 140 embassies, along with 665 consulates and four other diplomatic missions across the country.

Below are a few of the foreign embassies in Italy. For a full list, please visit the following website: https://www.embassypages.com/italy.

To report an incident involving a U.S. Citizen, contact the U.S. Embassy.

The U.S. Embassy
Palazzo Margherita
via Vittorio Veneto 121
00187 Roma
Tel: (+39) 06 46741
Website: https://it.usembassy.gov/

---

61 https://carpediemtours.com/blog/history-of-aperitivo/

To report an incident involving a Canadian Citizen, contact the Canadian Embassy.

The Canadian Embassy/Rome

Via Zara 30

Rome 00198

Tel: (+39) 06 85444 1

Website: https://www.international.gc.ca/country-pays/italy-italie

To report an emergency involving a Citizen of Brazil, contact the Brazilian Embassy.

The Brazilian Embassy

Piazza Navona 14

00186 Roma

Tel: (+39) 06 683 981

Website: https://www.brazil-embassy.net/br/Brazil-in-Rome

To report an emergency involving a Citizen of Switzerland, contact the Swiss Embassy.

The Swiss Embassy

Via Barnaba Oriani 61

00197 Roma

Tel: (+39) 06 809 571

Website: https://www.eda.admin.ch/countries/italy/it/home/rappresentanze/ambasciata-roma.html

To report an emergency involving a Citizen of Morocco, contact the Moroccan Embassy.

Moroccan Embassy

Via Brenta, 12/16

00198 Roma

Tel: (+39) 06 855 0801

Email: https://www.ambasciatamarocco.it/

To report an emergency involving a United Kingdom Citizen, contact the British Embassy.

British Embassy
Via XX Settembre 80a
00187 Roma
Tel: (+39) 06 4220 2333
Website: www.gov.uk/government/world/italy

To report an emergency involving a Citizen of Japan, contact the Japanese Embassy.

Japanese Embassy
Via Quintino Sella, 60
00187 Roma
Tel: (+39) 06 487 991
Website: https://www.it.emb-japan.go.jp/itprtop_it/b_000054.html

To report an emergency involving a Citizen of Germany, contact the German Embassy.

German Embassy
Via San Martino della Battaglia
4 00185 Roma
Tel: (+39) 06 49 213 1
Website: https://italien.diplo.de/

QUICK REFERENCE GUIDE

- Quick Chapter References to Important Topics

QUICK REFERENCE GUIDE

Crime in Italy

Are there particular areas in Italy that I should avoid as a tourist?

Yes. Be extra vigilant in Naples and Mezzogiorno in Southern Italy as they have higher crime rates. *For more details, see Chapter 3.*

Drug Offenses

Is recreational possession of marijuana legal in Italy?

No. *For more details, see Chapter 4.*

Is Delta 8 legal in Italy?

No. *For more details, see Chapter 4.*

Alcohol-Related Offenses

What is the legal drinking age in Italy?

18 is the legal drinking age.

What is the legal blood alcohol limit to drive in Italy?

The legal blood alcohol limit for driving in Italy is **0.5 g/liter,** and penalties for driving under the influence (DUI) apply once this limit is exceeded. *For more details, see Chapter 5.*

Firearm & Ammunition Offenses

Can I possess a gun?

No. In Italy, possessing a gun is regulated by strict rules and guns are banned without special permission. Even with permission, you can have it only at home, or use a gun for specific reasons like sports or hunting. Walking around armed is banned.

Can a tourist in Italy possess a stun gun?

No, the possession of a stun gun is strictly prohibited in Italy. *For more details, see Chapter 6.*

Prostitution

Is prostitution legal in Italy?

Yes. *For more details, see Chapter 7.*

LGBTQ

Is homosexuality legal in Italy?

Yes.

Are same sex marriages legal in Italy?

No, however Italy approved same-sex civil unions in 2016. *For more details, see Chapter 8.*

Arrested in Italy

Who should I notify if I am arrested in Italy?

You should notify your home country's embassy.

Will I be entitled to bail if I am arrested?

No, Italy does not offer bail. *For more details, see Chapter 10.*

Helping a Friend or Relative Imprisoned in Italy

Can I send money to a friend or family member imprisoned in Italy?

Yes, you can send money to a friend or relative who is imprisoned in Italy. However, there are specific procedures you must follow. *For more details, see Chapter 12.*

Crime Victim Assistance

Are there free translation services to assist me if I have to report a crime?

Yes, in Italy, the prosecuting authority will assign a translator to assist you. *For more details, see Chapter 14.*

Police

Is there an official state police force?

Yes, the Provincial Police (Polizia Provinciale) and the Municipal Police (Polizia Municipal). *For more details, see Chapter 15.*

Is there a number for a police emergency in Italy?

Yes, dial **112** in the event of a police emergency. *For more details, see Chapter 17.*

How to Get Legal Help in Italy

Is there a resource in Italy to find English-speaking legal representation?

Yes, visit **https://it.usembassy.gov/u-s-citizen-services/attorneys/** for a list of English-speaking attorneys in Italy. *For more details, see Chapter 16.*

Is pro bono free legal representation assistance offered in Italy?

Yes, legal aid is available to non-citizens in criminal cases, regardless of their immigration status or whether they are legally residing in Italy. *For more details, see Chapter 16.*

Medical Facilities & Hospitals

What is the number I can call in Italy for ambulance and fire emergencies?

Dial **118 for ambulance**, and **112 fire emergencies.** *For more details, see Chapter 17.*

Is there a list of hospitals I can refer to if I become ill or injured while in Italy?

Yes, there is a list of hospitals and healthcare facilities you can refer to, if you become ill or injured while in Italy. The Italian Ministry of Health provides information on public hospitals, and many embassies also offer a list of recommended hospitals for their citizens. *For more details, see Chapter 17.*

Driving in Italy

Can I use my driver's license from my home country to drive in Italy?

Yes, however, any license issued by a non-EU country is required to be accompanied by either an international driving permit OR a sworn translation of the license. *For more details, see Chapter 18.*

Which side of the road do I drive on in Italy?

Cars are driven on the right side of the road. *For more details, see Chapter 18.*

Nude Beaches & Clothing-Optional Resorts

Is nudity legal on the beaches?

Only on designated beaches. *For more details, see Chapter 19.*

Tourist Taxation

Is there a tourist tax in Italy?

Yes, Italian cities charge a local tourist tax, which is collected by the hotel where you are staying.

What affects the amount of tourist tax I have to pay?

The amount of tourist tax can vary based on the location and the length of your stay. *For more details, see Chapter 22.*

Long-Term Stays

As an American, how long can I stay in Italy without a formal visa?

Generally, as an American, you can stay in Italy for up to 3 months without a visa. *For more details, see Chapter 23.*

Practical Tips

What type of electrical sockets are used in Italy?

The common electrical socket used in Italy is 230 V AC, 50Hz-Type F. *For more details, see Chapter 25.*

In the Event of Death

Are there specific procedures for reporting the death of a US citizen in Italy?

Yes, the United States Embassy provides the procedures for reporting the death of a US citizen in Italy. *For more details, see Chapter 25.*

Foreign Embassies in Italy

Are there many foreign embassies in Italy?

Yes. The Italian capital Rome hosts 140 embassies, 665 consulates and three other representations.

Where can I locate embassies in Italy?

Visit **https://www.embassypages.com/italy**. *For more details, see Chapter 25.*

EMERGENCY/IMPORTANT CONTACT NUMBERS IN ITALY

 Please consider putting some of these numbers in your phone prior to traveling to Italy.

The most important emergency number to know is the NUE (Numero Unico Europeo), **112**, the single European emergency number. If you're in an emergency and can't recall any other numbers, 112 is your go-to. Whether you're facing a medical emergency, fire, crime, or even if you're lost in an Italian forest, dialing 112 will connect you to the nearest emergency service. The operators speak several languages, ensuring that help is always accessible.

For needs limited to specific areas, you can call the following numbers:

- **State Police:** 113 (accidents, thefts, etc.)
- **Fire Brigade:** 115 (fires, weather emergencies).
- **Urgent and emergency medical attention/ambulance:** 118
- **Red Cross Ambulance:** 5510
- **A.C.I. (Italian Automobile Club) Road Assistance:** 803 116.
- **Forest Ranger:** 1515
- **Travel Information:** 1518
- **Sea Rescue:** 1530
- Customs/Financial Police 117
- **Taxi:** 063570, 066645, 064994, 0688177 or 064157

- **Tourist Information:** 060608

Legal Assistance for Tourists
https://touristlegalassistance.com
touristlegalassistance1@gmail.com

Milan Bar Association
Via Carlo Freguglia 1, 20122 Milano (MI)
Tel. +39 02 5492921

USEFUL ITALIAN PHRASES

Greetings

HI/HELLO – Ciao

GOOD MORNING – Buongiorno

GOOD AFTERNOON – Buon pomeriggio

GOOD NIGHT – Buona notte

GOODBYE – Addio

Magic Words

PLEASE – Per favore

THANK YOU – Grazie

YOU'RE WELCOME – Prego

CHEERS! – Salute!

EXCUSE ME – Scusa/scusami

YES/NO – Sì/no

Getting Around

WHERE IS THE BATHROOM? – Dove è il bagno?

WHAT TIME IS IT? – Che ore sono?

HOW DO I GET TO...? – Come arrivo a...?

WHERE DOES THIS TRAIN/BUS GO? – Dove va questo treno/autobus?

RESTAURANT – Ristorante

HOW MUCH DOES THIS COST? – Quanto costa questo?

TRAIN/METRO STATION – Stazione ferroviaria/metropolitana

Communication

DO YOU SPEAK ENGLISH? – Parli inglese?

I DO NOT UNDERSTAND – Non capisco

I DON'T SPEAK ITALIAN – Non parlo italiano

I DON'T KNOW – Non so

Emergency

HELP! – Aiuto!

CALL AN AMBULANCE! – Chiama un'ambulanza!

I NEED A DOCTOR – Ho bisogno di un medico

POLICE – Polizia

I'M LOST – Sono perso/a

IT'S AN EMERGENCY – È un'emergenza

GLOSSARY

ACQUITTAL: A jury verdict that a criminal defendant is not guilty, or the finding of a judge that the evidence cannot support a conviction.

ADVERSARY PROCEEDING: A lawsuit arising from a controversy that begins with filing a complaint.

AFFIDAVIT: A written statement made under oath.

APPEAL: A request made after a trial court has decided against one party in which the losing party asks a higher court to review the decision for legal error.

ARRAIGNMENT: A proceeding in which a criminal defendant is brought to court, told of the charges, and asked to plead guilty or not guilty.

BAIL: The temporary release of a person from jail when awaiting trial, on thecondition that a sum of money be lodged or deposited to guarantee an appearance in court.

BARRISTER: A lawyer admitted to plead at the Bar and who may try cases in superior court.

BURDEN OF PROOF: The duty to prove disputed facts.

CAUSE OF ACTION: A legal claim in a civil action.

COMPLAINT: A written statement that begins a civil lawsuit in which the plaintiff details the claims.

CONTRACT: An agreement between two or more persons to do something or to not do something.

CONVICTION: A judgment of guilt against a person charged with a crime.

CUSTOMS DUTY: A tariff or tax imposed on goods when transported across international borders.

COURT LIAISON: A person that coordinates with attorneys to perform administrative duties, such as scheduling witnesses, sharing information with law enforcement, and overseeing the reporting of cases to foreign embassies when applicable.

DAMAGES: Money that a defendant pays to a plaintiff in a civil case if the plaintiff wins.

DEFENDANT: 1) The individual against whom a civil claim is filed; 2) The individual against whom a criminal charge is filed.

FELONY: A serious crime, punishable by more than one year in prison.

MAGISTRATE: A judicial officer of a district court, who conducts initial proceedings in criminal cases, decides criminal misdemeanor cases, conducts many pretrial civil and criminal matters on behalf of district judges, and decides civil cases with the consent of the parties.

MISDEMEANOR: An offense punishable by one year or less in jail.

PLAINTIFF: A person or business that files a formal civil complaint with the court.

PLEA: In a criminal case, the answer of "guilty," "not guilty," or "no contest" in response to a criminal charge.

SOLICITOR: A lawyer who advises clients, represents them in lower court, and prepares cases for barristers to try in higher courts.

SOVEREIGN IMMUNITY: A legal doctrine by which the sovereign or the state (i.e. government) cannot commit a legal wrong, and thus, it is immune from criminal and civil liability and cannot be sued.

STATUTE: A written law passed by a legislative body.

STATUTE OF LIMITATIONS. A statute prescribing a period of limitation to bring certain types of legal actions. If the action is not brought within that time, the person or entity (in a criminal context) is permanently barred from suing in court.

SUBPOENA: A command, issued under court authority, for a witness to appear and to give testimony.

TESTIMONY: Evidence presented orally by witnesses.

VERDICT: The decision of a judge or jury in a case.

WARRANT: Court authorization to conduct a search or to make an arrest.

ACKNOWLEDGMENTS

This book series would never have seen the light of day without the able assistance of the following people:

Kathy Adams, my paralegal for over 22 years, who is the "Best" I've ever worked with during my entire legal career because of her amazing work ethic, organizational skills, and her ability to think outside of the box in unique and creative ways;

Ally Knez-Siddique, a professional writer, and one of my paralegals, whose eye for detail, according to her, is both a blessing and a curse;

Rosa Diaz Graham, my legal assistant who helped with research and word processing at the very beginning of this project;

Mindy Scarlett, my marketing and publishing "Guru"! Her creativity and vision have no boundaries!

ABOUT THE AUTHOR

Michael L. Moore practices in Orlando, Florida, the city where he spent his formative years. He credits the trauma of having his brother murdered when he was only 10 years old, as the catalyst that drew him into the practice of law.

Moore attended Florida State University, where he was a member of the FSU debate team. Upon graduating, he was awarded a full scholarship to attend the University of Tennessee College of Law, where he was elected President of the Student Bar Association. He further honed his advocacy and public speaking skills by participating in 'moot court' competitions.

After clerking at the Tennessee Attorney General's office while in law school, Moore moved back to Orlando, Florida, to work at the State Attorney's Office as a prosecutor, and where he was fortunate enough to meet the young lady that would eventually become his wife. Moore moved on to working for private law firms, both local and national, and eventually established his own law firm in 1999. He continues to make Orlando his home base.

It was the murder of a close friend and client in Jamaica that caused Moore to realize that books on laws in other countries were few and far between, and he was inspired to create Law of the Land Publishing. Moore launched Law of the Land Publishing to provide a series of guide-books and a membership site for tourists and business travelers to stay up to date on the laws in each country they travel to, as well as having access to assistance if they run into legal issues.

"My vision is to educate people on what their legal rights are, and how they can access legal assistance, no matter where they have to travel to in the world," said Moore. "As Americans, we have a right to due process, but in some countries, you don't even have the right to access a square meal when incarcerated. My goal is to provide the information needed to stay out of trouble, as well as having access to assistance if trouble finds you."

www.ingramcontent.com/pod-product-compliance
Lightning Source LLC
Chambersburg PA
CBHW041625140626
46547CB00030B/934